A Step-by-Step Guide for Teachers, Therapists and Parents

Calm & Alert

Yoga and Mindfulness Practices to
Teach Self-regulation & Social Skills to Children

Helene McGlauflin, MEd,LCPC,KYT
Foreword by Peg Dawson

Calm and Alert
Copyright © 2018 by Helene McGlauflin

Published by
PESI Publishing & Media
PESI, Inc
3839 White Ave
Eau Claire, WI 54703

Cover: Amy Rubenzer
Editing: Joy Hurlburt
Layout: Amy Rubenzer & Bookmasters
ISBN: 9781683731320
All rights reserved.
Printed in the United States of America.

PESI
Publishing
& Media
www.pesi.com

Dedication

This book is dedicated to my grandchildren
and all present and future children on our planet.

May they be healthy
May they be conscious
May they be strong and resilient

Table of Contents

Chapters

Acknowledgements

I wish to thank:

Karsyn Morse, and all the editors at PESI, who accepted my work for publication and brought it to fruition.

My colleagues, family, and friends who have always supported my work, allowing it to develop with their willingness, input, and faith. This includes the educators who have helped develop *Calm and Alert* since the beginning: Beth Cowing-Young, Jennifer Greenleaf, Mary Belanger, Dot Bowie, Barb Morrill, Sarah Morrill, Sandy Horrocks, Lona Anagnostis, Sandy Michaud, Rob Horne, Donna Tardif, Alison Guite, Lonie Ellis, Chris LaJoie, Karen Totman, and Rick Dedek. It also includes those who have been supporters, readers, and research participants: Danika Kuhl, Sara Eaton, Erica Alt, Barb Picarillo, Brian McPherson, Meggin Farrell, Sarah Patton, Sydney Perkins, Kristen Klaiber, Marybeth Brown, Elin Goodwin, Vicky Dow, Krista Walker, Erin Dimbleby, Katie Gould, Amy Hall, Corrie Scribner, Tanji Johnston, Naomi Mullane, Terry Cullison, Conor McGlauflin, Molly McGlauflin Kroiz, Bruce McGlauflin, Jeff Morrill, Marita O'Neill, Katherine Bynes, Peg Dawson.

All the wonderful yoga teachers I have had, and do have, especially Leslie Simmons, my first and most revered teacher, and all the fine teachers at the Kriplau Center for Yoga and Health.

All the children who have practiced with me, helping *Calm and Alert* grow.

Mother Teresa of Calcutta, whose words: "We cannot do great things. We can only do small things with great love," have sustained me each day in my work.

About the Author

 **Helene McGlauflin**, MEd, LCPC, KYT, is a counselor, writer and yoga teacher. She holds a Masters Degree in Counselor Education from the University of Southern Maine, is a Licensed Clinical Professional Counselor in the state of Maine and a certified Kripalu Yoga Teacher.

Helene has worked with and for children and those who raise and serve them for 30 years. Over the course of her career she has had experience as a special education teacher, a school counselor, a consultant and trainer in the field of grief and loss, an adjunct professor of child development, and a yoga teacher. She has dedicated much of her career to serving children as a school counselor in public schools in Midcoast Maine, but also spent many years training volunteers at the Center for Grieving Children in Portland, Maine, and teaching courses at the University of Southern Maine. Helene's training as a yoga teacher has allowed her the great pleasure of bringing the optimism and resiliency the practices offer to all the children, educators, and parents she has the privilege to serve.

She has always contributed to the fields her professional path has taken her through her writing. Helene has published over 30 articles and two booklets in professional journals, magazines, books, small presses and online resources concerning children and how to support them in their social/emotional development, their grieving, and their resiliency. Helene's writing can be found in the field of school counseling, in journals such as *Professional School Counseling* and books such as *Counselors Finding Their Way*; the field of grief and loss in journals such as *American Journal of Hospice Care*, and her booklets *Supporting Children and Teens through Grief and Loss* (one for parents and one for schools); the field of parent support in publications such as *Mothering Magazine and Renewal: A Journal for Waldorf Education;* and now with the publication of *Calm and Alert*, the field of yoga and mindfulness for children. Helene is also a poet with two published books: *Tiny Sabbath* (2010) and *Teacher I Honor You: Poems Honoring Young People, Parents and Teachers* (2016).

Helene lives with her husband, Bruce, in Midcoast Maine, and holds most precious her two grown children, Molly and Conor, their spouses, Sam and Hannah, and her grandchildren, Mabel and Doolin.

Find *Calm and Alert* online at calmandalert.com. Helene would love to hear from you at calmandalert@gmail.com.

Foreword

I became interested in mindfulness meditation many years ago, but it took me the longest time to investigate it as a viable option for helping children struggling with behavioral and emotional regulation. When I began seeing citations to research articles that claimed that "mindfulness meditation improves executive functioning," I knew I couldn't avoid the subject any longer. As an "expert" on executive skills and the co-author of several books on the topic written for parents and educators (e.g., *Smart but Scattered, Executive Skills in Children and Adolescents*), I finally decided I needed to understand the practice of mindfulness meditation better. So I began delving into the research and began exploring the practice for myself (using a smartphone app that I love called *Headspace*).

Helene McGlauflin and I have a friendship that goes back a long way, and I've followed her career as a school counselor from her early years. When she began talking about her *Calm and Alert* program, a program that integrates yoga and mindfulness with skill building, I viewed it initially as a great way for her to reach more children than school counselors are typically able to do if they are seeing kids one at a time in their office. Helene and I typically see each other just a few times a year, and over the years she would share with me her experiences developing this program to help children learn to better regulate their feelings and activity level. She always seemed hopeful yet realistic about the impact of her work on the lives of children.

When I started making the connection between meditation and executive skills, I became more interested in Helene's work. I was asked to do a workshop on executive skills in New Hampshire, and I assembled people throughout New England who were using diverse methods for helping children improve these skills in a school setting. Helene was one of the people I invited; and in the short period of time allotted to her on the program, she shared her methodology and had the audience practice some of the techniques she was using. And when she began to talk about writing an instructor's manual for *Calm and Alert*, I encouraged her to pursue this. This book is the culmination of her efforts, and I couldn't be more excited knowing that her program can now reach a larger audience.

Helene is already a published author. She's written several books of poetry, and when you begin to read this manual, you will see that influence. She finds a way of describing children and explaining her practice using words that remind you of the essential goodness and dignity of humanity. But she also gently reminds us that in the 21st century, with exposure to so much stimulation, a fast-paced world, all kinds of technology at one's fingertips, and parents who have more to manage than they can comfortably fit into a day, many children don't know what it feels like to be either calm or alert. Her program teaches children to access both those feelings. But it goes beyond that, in that it is constructed around routines that help children learn to function in social groups and learn to self-regulate when confronted with a wide variety of stressors.

Helene teaches patience, both with yourself as an instructor and with the techniques you are using. Interventions are all too often boiled down to a formula: bi-weekly 30-minute sessions for eight weeks. That fits a typical research protocol, but it doesn't match up well with what we know about behavior change or habit formation. Both of these involve lots of practice over time. In my work with parents and teachers, I often tell them, "Progress is measured in years and not months." While I often do see progress in months (and Helene attests to that in the case examples in this manual), this message preaches patience. Particularly with children who struggle mightily with emotional regulation, we don't want to give up too quickly on strategies that have a high probability of success if people would only give them time to work.

Here are some other things I like about this manual. It's user-friendly in its format. While the program is sequential, it's also recursive, in that Helene returns in later sessions to techniques and terms introduced in earlier sessions. She doesn't make you go back and track down those original references. Rather, each chapter stands on its own, and if something needs to be retrieved from an earlier lesson, Helene retrieves it for you.

Each lesson depicts a set of activities that are carefully thought-out and arranged in a sequence that makes sense. The whole process is economical in that Helene is able to point out how learning routines, such has how to care for mats or how to sit in groups, are actually part of the learning process and not just steps to be taken care of quickly so that the lesson can be taught efficiently.

I love the way she builds all these activities around three centers, body, mind, and breath, and three concepts or attitudes, respect, calm, and alert. And she has simple, elegant ways of explaining each of these to children. A calm breath is "slow and deep," she tells us; an alert breath is "quick in, quick out." The mind is something that can be trained, so that your thoughts are "clear rather than muddy." And a body that feels best is one that is "safe and in control."

She also offers suggestions for adapting her methods to individual children and to settings other than schools. She describes in knowing detail how children with ADHD or oppositional behavior, or children on the autism spectrum are likely to react to *Calm and Alert*. And she provides practical suggestions for modifying the lessons to fit those children who are more behaviorally challenged. She even suggests ways parents can adapt lessons for use in the home.

And finally, this manual is the culmination of years of learning how the process works. Her rich experience shines through on every page. She tells the novice instructor what to expect, where problems may arise, and how to handle glitches as they come up. All written in a "calm voice" that communicates to the reader: This may not be easy, particularly in the beginning, but it is worth working at. I finished her book thinking that learning her techniques would not only benefit the children who are the intended audience, but would prove immensely valuable to the adults who want to learn to do what Helene has done over the decades with hundreds of children.

I trust that readers who follow the instructions in this manual in their work with children will see the benefits. I am confident that with this program children will become able to better navigate a world fraught with uncertainty by learning to control their mind, body, and breath, and in so doing increase their capacity to feel calm and alert no matter the situation.

Peg Dawson, Ed.D., NCSP
author of *Smart but Scattered*

Welcome to Calm & Alert

Every year I have had the privilege of standing in front of an elementary school to greet the students and families on the first day of school. Stand with me today and see the scene: a crisp New England September day, sun shining, cool breeze. Some parents show up early with their cameras, awaiting the bus, others with hands tightly holding their child's. There are children walking in on their own, those with one parent, or those with an extended family around them and, soon, children on the bus, some whose parents rarely come to school. There are little girls in their best dresses, and little boys in ties; there are children who seem to have rolled out of bed just five minutes before, with disheveled hair and unmatched clothing. Many emotions are evident through smiles, tears, children clinging to or proudly running from their parents, and children with blank, unreadable faces.

The first bus rolls up and squeaks to a halt, the doors flap open and the littlest ones slowly come down the steps. Some are shy and unsure, others bold and confident. A little girl in freshly combed pigtails and a matching outfit comes up to us smiling shyly. She smells of soap. You lean down and ask her name and she says, "Julie. I don't know where to go." You help her find her way and she looks relieved. You turn toward the bus again and see a little boy with dark matted hair hanging in his eyes, and clothes that are not new staring up at the outside of the school, seemingly in awe. You walk toward him, noting the lingering smell of cigarette smoke as you approach. He blurts out, "My name is Jimmy and I live in a trailer." You welcome him and help him find his place in line behind Julie.

After multiple large buses come and go, next come smaller buses and vans. The first small bus pulls up and a wide door opens and a ramp shoots out and down, allowing a wheelchair-using child to buzz out in her electric chair. Four other students use the door with steps. One boy has an unusual gait and finds the stairs very difficult but is remarkably adept at swinging his legs rhythmically to help him down the steps. He has a broad smile and with a slurring cadence tells me his name, Phillip. Another child shows little recognition of the people greeting her. The third darts out and away in a concerning manner until an adult steps in for safety. Another cautiously taps his cane in front of him to feel his way to our doors. Phillip is able to join the line with support; the other students are led to other special education classrooms with assistance.

We have just welcomed a microcosm of U.S. society into our halls, with the responsibility of teaching each of them to read, write, master math, science, social studies, and social skills in the freest, most appropriate way we can. Each child, in order to learn most ably, will be expected to communicate with their teacher and their classmates, follow rules and directions, listen, focus and attend, complete work, show self-control, cooperate, share, wait, take care of their belongings, sing, run, treat materials and others with respect, eat politely, ask for help when needed, make and keep friends. All of the above will require a general capacity to regulate their bodies, thoughts, words, and emotions.

How successful will they be? What will their futures hold? In my experience in the current school and national culture, it is hard to predict. It would be easy to jump to the supposition that Julie will do well, Jimmy not so well, and Phillip will need considerable support. Certainly, Julie's basic needs for clothing, food, and shelter appear to be met and will provide a solid foundation; Jimmy might arrive hungry and have had few educational experiences. Phillip's physical challenges will need to be accommodated. But in the 21st century, all three children will find many demands placed on their developing brains and bodies, and each will most likely find a number of skill areas challenging. They all will need explicit instruction in the many skills that relate to self-management, learning, social interactions, work attitudes and completion, and behaving appropriately in order to successfully navigate their way through school and be foundationally prepared for success in any setting.

***Calm and Alert* was developed and designed to help all children master foundational skills they need for success in the 21st century**. It has developed since the turn of the century, when the research on using yoga and mindfulness with children to teach self-regulation and social skills was very new and very promising. *Calm and Alert* contributes to this nascent field by drawing from research-based practices from the fields of social/emotional learning, yoga with children, mindfulness with children, and self-regulation in children. It is designed to weave these fields together and bring the practices comfortably to all children and those who serve them by creating concepts and defining skills that are firmly grounded in the research from relevant fields. The program's practices are offered freely, are completely secular, and have been noncontroversial. My hope is to validate seasoned yoga and mindfulness enthusiasts, encourage beginners, comfort the cautious, and satisfy those seeking evidence-based practices. (See Appendix 3 for research support.)

Calm and Alert was developed and designed through my years of inquiry and concern for the hundreds of children I serve each year, who increasingly were struggling to develop the self-regulation needed to master the complex social skills required by modern living in multiple settings. These include:

- Listening
- Focus
- Following directions
- Being appropriate in groups
- Resolving conflicts
- Showing empathy
- Being organized

- Showing respect and kindness
- Being responsible
- Initiating tasks
- Showing physical control
- Showing emotional control
- Flexibility

The importance of such skills on school and life success is well documented in the literature and most conclude that children without such skills are at risk for numerous school and life difficulties or failures, so the situation was urgent. The traditional methods of teaching self-regulation and social skills (modeling, role playing, positive reinforcement), though beneficial, were not quite enough anymore. I was seeking something more fundamental. I wanted a more explicit method for helping children develop internal self-awareness and the mind-body states that encourage self-regulation.

The field of yoga, which requires children to engage their bodies, minds, and breath simultaneously through movement, and the field of mindfulness, which requires children to bring focused attention without judgment to every task, have offered me the best tools for teaching self-regulation of these social skills in the most explicit way. I sought extensive training through the 200-hour Kripalu Yoga Teacher Training (2008) and 40-hour YogaEd Curriculum Training (2010) and have a long-established personal practice which enabled me to competently integrate this field into my teaching. To contribute to the field myself, I conducted an action research pilot study at my school site on the *Calm and Alert* class (McGlauflin, 2010), which sought feedback from both parents and teachers, and also had a social work intern conduct a case study of its effectiveness (Perkins, 2015).

Articles that discuss teaching yoga skills to children have shown general promise in offering children explicit tools for being "calm and alert," but attempt to measure a wide range of variables. These variables include, but are not limited to, improvements in:

- Health, well-being, and mood
- Academic achievement and school success
- Self-regulation
- Anxiety and stress reduction
- Improvements in ability to focus and attend

What I have seen that is not yet reflected in the research is the improvement in self-awareness, controlled movement, and pride in better functioning.

I have selected the safest and most comfortably secular aspects from the yoga field to bring to the *Calm and Alert* practices. These include a deep respect for teaching and learning, creating a partnership between teacher and child; the instruction in, and practice of, mindful movement and conscious breathing; the relaxed, calming atmosphere the practices encourage; the imagery from nature; the partnership between body, mind, and breath; and the principles of healthy exertion and rest. Throughout the practice, children should be happy, relaxed even when challenged, their minds and bodies feeling free. These elements from the yoga field have been more enjoyable to the children and more effective instruction than I ever imagined.

Articles that discuss teaching mindfulness to children also show general promise in offering students concrete tools (meditation, breathing exercises, instruction about how the brain works) to be conscious of their bodies and minds and develop self-regulation. Mindfulness research reports improvements for children in areas of:

- Overall health
- School success
- Self-regulation
- Attention
- Anxiety reduction
- Prevention of self-harm
- On-task behavior in the classroom
- Improved executive function

This field also offers research support that mindfulness practices can help reduce stress for teachers and thereby offer benefits for the children they serve, which I hear regularly from teachers.

I have also selected the safest and least controversial aspects from the mindfulness field to bring to the *Calm and Alert* practices, such as the benefits of utilizing the breath for creating calm and alert states, noticing the workings of the mind, attention and focus skills, and teaching children about their brains. The beauty of the mindfulness practices are that they do not require movement for adults who are not confident or inclined, and they are easy to implement in any setting. A few conscious breaths can be done anywhere, attentional strategies are useful for any task, and children enjoy learning and talking about the workings of the brain.

The well-established field of social/emotional learning that has long looked at the development of social skills, effective teaching practices, and evidence-based curriculums has helped shape *Calm and Alert* lessons. I have ensured the classes are sequenced, active, focused, and explicit (SAFE):

Sequenced: As outlined in the chapters, skills can build on one another.

Active: The learning involves movement and the awareness of the body.

Focused: Children are fully engaged and are taught how to engage and focus in each area.

Explicit: Skills are clearly defined, expectations clearly stated in each area, and movements/breathwork are taught step-by-step.

Recognizing the importance of establishing core program components in this field, *Calm and Alert* offers six concept/unit areas (respect, calm, alert, learning times, transition times, social times) for instruction.

The field of self-regulation has offered *Calm and Alert* a developmental perspective on the importance of practice for mastery, the repetition of practice needed for "effortful control" to develop, and the concepts of physiological states that are helpful in learning. The terms "calm" or "alert" are found at regular intervals in the literature, recognized as optimal states for best learning and functioning. These *Calm and Alert* terms have been catchy and comfortable for children and adults in a public school setting, and the six unit areas are a comprehensive way to respect the recommendations of this field.

This journey with *Calm and Alert* has been exciting and troubling: Exciting because I have seen the *Calm and Alert* practices effectively help hundreds of children in the last 12 years be happier, more successful, and resilient at home and school; troubling because the demands and ensuing stress I see placed on our children in school, at home, in cyberspace, and in other real-time activities seems at times developmentally inappropriate. Though many children rise to the occasion, I wonder about the cost to their developing bodies, minds, and hearts.

That said, I take an optimistic stand: **We can always respond to the needs of our children and our times with innovation and flexibility.** *Calm and Alert* has allowed me to maintain and offer this optimism to the children, teachers, parents, and other adults who serve young people. Our children today learn social skills and regulation by using their minds, bodies, and senses, by explicit instruction, practice, and through fun. *Calm and Alert* offers children these things and so much more. My intention in writing this book is to offer a practical and useable guide to help those who read it stay hopeful and inspired to shape our children into the resilient adults and responsible citizens who will help us face our collective future.

My intention here was to introduce you to the need, roots, and research relevant to the development of *Calm and Alert*, and to place it in this emerging field. When I teach it as a class, I begin by speaking to the children as they sit at their seats about what we are about to do and share. We sing a song and then prepare to move the furniture to make room for our practice. I have been speaking to you as you sit in your seat until this moment.

Join me now in taking a deep breath; get ready to move your internal furniture and make room for the inspiration of practice.

How to Use this Book

Whether you're a teacher, therapist, parent, or other profession that serves children, this book can serve you. I want this book to inspire you, but also give you the practical tools to teach children how to be respectful, calm, alert, and clear about the expectations for learning, transitioning between activities, and socializing. **After the basic introduction to *Calm and Alert*, I've included six chapters that address the following:**

Chapter 2: Respect

Chapter 3: Calm

Chapter 4: Alert

Chapter 5: Learning Time

Chapter 6: Transition Time

Chapter 7: Social Time

For ease, all these chapters are structured similarly and all offer the specific exercises and strategies to teach children on the given topic. These lessons are realistic and easy to implement in any setting and I hope you will find the ideas and methods clear and simple. Depending on your role, you can turn to the section appropriate for your needs.

Chapter 8 deviates from the structure in Chapters 1–7 to discuss evidence of the effectiveness of *Calm and Alert*. The chapter is organized using a very simplified version of a framework that has helped many public schools discuss how to think about and teach all their children, depending on their skill level and how they respond to instruction, using the concept of tiers on a triangle. The basic headings of the chapter are organized by numbered tiers, and the subsections allow readers interested in measurement tools to find what they are looking for in "measuring the fruits" and those wishing to see the effects through personal accounts to find what they are looking for in "seeing the fruits."

Structure of Each Chapter

Aside from the final chapter, all chapters offer the following repetitious organizational framework to create a rhythm for use:

Song/Poem. Each chapter opens with the words to the *Calm and Alert* song/poem that can be used with younger children to introduce and explain the concept and skills of the concept area as you to begin.

Exploration of Chapter Topic. Each chapter then offers a brief introduction to the topic, giving you the rationale for the topic and insights about how the topic came to be developed. My intention is to be encouraging and supportive. A number of my particular word definitions and perspectives may be new to any reader, and so provide an essential foundation for the chapter.

Chapter Concepts. This section briefly outlines the vocabulary for the chapter, an "at a glance" reference for you. When needed, this is supported by a brief defense of how and why the concepts are defined and taught in this particular way.

Teaching Calm and Alert as a Class. This section of each chapter offers you the framework for teaching the skills as a 30–40 minute lesson suitable for a classroom or small group of children in another setting. These lessons have been taught to both children with special challenges, typically developing peers, and both groups together. These lessons can be taught by a classroom teacher, a yoga teacher, or therapist. A lesson template/overview is also offered.

Teaching and Using Calm and Alert in Other Settings. This section of each chapter is designed for occupational therapists, physical therapists, speech therapists, mental health professionals, or yoga/mindfulness teachers who may use *Calm and Alert* in an alternative classroom, office, or studio setting. These noble practitioners more regularly serve students with unique challenges, disabilities, or special needs, such as:

- Autism
- Anxiety
- Anger management
- Sensory issues
- Behavior challenges
- ADHD and executive function (EF) deficits
- Developmental delays

Calm and Alert can serve these populations, both in a classroom setting or an office/studio with modifications and special considerations. So while this section is designed with therapists in mind, it can also be used as a reference for a teacher facing special challenges with particular students. This section will highlight the foundational concepts of the chapter, with these subsections:

In **recommended essentials**, the fundamentals will be distilled, such as "if you only have this much time, this much space, or these challenges, keep a primary focus on these essentials for skill development." I have come to see that here, in the recommended essentials for each chapter, you find the simple power of the practices. These can be enough for any child, and can provide small, realistic benefits for children with special needs or other challenges.

In **modifying class elements**, each of the seven class components will be reviewed with special populations in mind, but could also be a help to a teacher struggling with a particularly challenging class. The reassuring message of this section is: These practices are mastered over time, gently, internally, and the process cannot be rushed.

Teaching and Using Calm and Alert at Home. This section of each chapter is for parents and caregivers who want to encourage *Calm and Alert* at home. The **recommended essentials** in this section will highlight simple practices anyone at any skill level can feel confident using with children of any skill level, with practical suggestions for breathing, movements, and language that can help cue children to utilize the skills. I hold a utopian view of a world in which every family has a zen chime they use regularly, every child and parent knows to take a calm breath when upset, and family members say to one another "you need to change those muddy thoughts to clear" when there is a seemingly intractable problem.

Chapter ONE
Calm and Alert Concepts

Being calm and alert makes most things easier. **A person who is calm is quiet and steady inside and out.** He/she is better able to navigate relationships with adults and peers, work through problems and solve them, think more clearly, and function more optimally. **A person who is alert is awake and ready to learn or perform a task.** He/she is better able to pay attention to themselves and the world around them, is careful with their body and words, and is responsive to the world. Being the opposite, overreactive and lethargic, makes everything harder: Tasks are more difficult, relationships can suffer, and problems increase. Our bodies, our minds, and our breath can help us become and stay calm and alert throughout the day in any setting.

The *Calm and Alert* basic concepts, skills, components, and lesson structure grew out of my desire to create short (30–40 minute) lessons or frameworks that would explicitly teach children, at every step, conscious use of the body, the mind, and the breath for these calm and alert states to be used at various times of the day. This helps children learn and experience the states in order to self-regulate and use their social skills most effectively. To that end, I knew that all the learning should offer a multisensory experience and require that children engage their bodies, minds, and breath as much as possible to optimize skill development through the concrete practices offered by the yoga and mindfulness fields. The practicing is the path to internal self-awareness, discovering the calm and alert states, and the generalization of skills at all times, in all settings: home, school, community.

I want children to feel excited about the fact that their bodies, their minds, and their breath can help them and are available every minute of every day. When successful, this excitement can be a seed for motivation to use the skills throughout the day in various settings. It encourages children to learn that their locus of control is themselves and can be shaped and changed: You have the power to control how you move, how you think, and how you breathe, and this affects how you feel. When you consciously choose to do so, that is the practice of self-regulation.

For some teachers/therapists/parents and children, this is a new way of approaching children. We are used to the idea that an adult controls and directs all children do, and the adult is responsible for everything that happens in a classroom, at home or other settings. Although often accurate, how much easier to consider and encourage a partnership between adult and child, in which children have the tools to choose what they need for the expectations at hand, such as an in-control body, a ready-to-learn mind, and the constancy of breath keeping them calm and alert? The adult scaffolds learning with structure and holds the environment steady while the children regulate themselves for learning. This vision is possible with these tools and frequent practice.

The Basics

| Body | Mind | Breath |

Body, Mind, Breath Concepts

My body is my helper when it's in control.
My mind is my helper when it's ready to learn.
My breath is my helper when it's calm and alert.

My body, mind, and breath help me
be successful every minute of every day.

Many modern children are unaware of their bodies and how they function, their minds and how they affect everything they say and do, and their breath coming in and out of their bodies continuously. So the basics must include explicit information about their bodies, minds, and breath; explicit exploration of their bodies, minds, and breath; and explicit practice in conscious use of all three.

Body. Your body is every part of you and is in your control. Being in control is expected; being out of control is unexpected and unacceptable. When we are in control we feel better, learn better, perform better, and have better relationships with peers and adults.

Body

Safe and in control

Mind. Your mind includes your brain and all it can do—thoughts (words) and pictures (images)—and your brain is constantly making both. You can train and change your thoughts and images. Thoughts/images that help you are clear and positive, and are healthy. Thoughts/images that hinder you are muddy and negative, and are unhealthy.

Mind

Clear rather than muddy
Positive rather than negative

Breath. Your breath describes the air coming in and going out of your lungs. It happens every minute of every day and keeps us alive whether we pay attention to it or not. But we can consciously pay attention to it to help ourselves. Calm breaths are slow and deep and alert breaths are quick and more forceful. We should try to be calm and alert for learning and optimal functioning in any setting.

Breath

Calm: slow and deep
Alert: quick in, quick out

The concepts of being respectful, calm, and alert each day grew from a noticeable need in these areas for many children. There are children who are *not* respectful, calm, and alert, unable to easily show caring to themselves, others, and things; who are agitated, reactive, and lack control; who are tired, lethargic, and unable to focus and attend. For these children, the attitude of respect and the calm/alert states are needed as a foundation to navigate any environment, or they will find situations at home or school difficult and discouraging by advertently or inadvertently not following rules, developing conflicts, or being unsafe. For children who are easily respectful, calm, and alert, the instruction provides validation, frequent positive feedback, and ease of practice.

Defining respect, calm, and alert for explicit instruction using body, mind, and breath has been challenging, though we may commonly overuse these words with children. The following definitions have been effective for even young children, and were developed through inquiry into the meaning of the words, the skill deficits needing to be addressed, and the practical need for concrete simplicity for instructing all types of children.

Respect. Respect means being caring, gentle, and serious with yourself, others, and all things at home, at school, and in the community. This includes your body, thoughts, and feelings; the body, thoughts, and feelings of others; and all things used in the physical world.

Respect

Caring = you never harm self, others, or things
Gentle = you are careful, helpful, and kind
Serious = all you say and do matters

I treat myself, others, and all things with
respect at all times.

Calm. Calm means being quiet and steady with your body, mind, and breath. Quiet is taught as still inside and out, without talking or noises. Steady is taught as anchored and in control. Of course, even the calmest child is wiggly, noisy when appropriate, and occasionally out of control! But from a skill development perspective, a child with a calm body is still and in control; a child with a calm mind can focus on the most important thing at hand and ignore distractions; a child with a calm breathing pattern has a steady inhale and exhale.

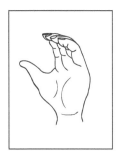

Calm
―――

Quiet = still, with no talking or noises
Steady = grounded and in control

I can be or become calm no matter
what happens.

Alert. Alert means awake and ready to learn or to perform a task at hand. Awake is taught as having your spine straight, eyes open, and being attentive to what is being taught, shown, happening, or required. Ready means you are prepared, willing, and your mind is "on" not "off."

Alert
―――

Awake = eyes open, sitting straight
Ready = prepared and willing

I can be alert or become alert
when needed.

Three Times of the Day Concepts

Framing a day by three "times" with expectations and understandings of the distinctive features of each "time" grew from a need to provide more instruction to children about what is expected at various times of the day. It was not new to teach children about transition times, often targeted as prime time for mindfulness or yoga, but there has been a need to categorize the other times of the day. These concepts can be generalized to all parts of a child's world as well: home, school, daycare, etc.

The three times of the day concepts have provided effective vocabulary for establishing expectations, and can help clarify for children they have a "job" in making whatever setting they are in a better place. Some ways of explaining this in various settings can be:

Your Job

Your job at school is to learn.
Your job at home is to be a loving, caring family member.
Your job at daycare is to be a respectful community member.
Your job on your team is to be a fair and helpful player.

Learning times. Learning times are when anyone is teaching something, anytime a child is expected to learn, work on a task, or practice something, often involving effort. Most times of the school day are learning times, and in modern society many after-school times at home and in the community are expected learning times. At structured learning times, children are expected to listen, focus, and follow the directions needed for their work or task. This helps to create a partnership between the person teaching and the learner.

Learning Time

Any time someone is teaching something. Any time a child is expected to learn, work on a task, or practice something, often involving effort.

Skills needed = listening, focusing, following directions

Transition times. Transition times are times when things change: An in-between time when we go from one thing to another. There are many, many daily transition times in the life of a modern child: waking up; getting ready in the morning; going to and leaving school, daycare, or other activities; between subjects and during a subject in school; mealtimes; going from indoors to outdoors—to name a few! At transition times, children can learn to be steady, careful, and focused, and so help transitions be smoother.

Transition Time

A time of change;
an in-between time when we go
from one thing to another.

Skills needed = steady, careful, focused

Social times. Social times are the times for friends and family when we are eating, talking freely or playing. In most classes and schools, social times are lunch, recess, and possibly snack or choice times. Outside of school these would be times with family and friends, such as play dates, parties, playing in the neighborhood, or community events. Children are expected to be safe with their words and bodies and regularly practice kindness.

Social Time

A time for friends and
family when we are eating,
talking freely, or playing.

Skills needed = safe and kind

Calm and Alert Materials Used Regularly

Materials referenced throughout the book help enhance the teaching of the skills by creating visuals for children, and increase engagement. Explanations for use of the materials will unfold as the book proceeds. If yours is a low or no budget operation, be comforted knowing that these materials are low cost and lasting, reproducibles are offered, and the skills can be taught without them. For example: Any person can make the sound of a chime which children can learn to listen to, but having a chime creates a visual and a musical instrument partner for you; mats are not necessary, but become special to children and offer an invaluable tool for teaching.

Recommended Materials

- Hoberman mini sphere (breathing ball)
- Zen chime
- Mind, body, breath cubes/icons
- Two small mason jars: one with mud, one with clear water
- Yoga mats, cut to size
- Bin to keep the rolled-up mats in
- Picture of the spine
- Pictures of six basic feelings: happy, sad, angry, scared, surprised, disgusted
- On/off switch

Teaching Calm and Alert as a Class

The basic class components are discussed in depth here and then more succinctly listed and summarized in the following class structure section. As a class, *Calm and Alert* can be taught in a public or private school classroom, a yoga studio, a childcare site or after-school activity, and in small or large groups.

The class components utilize a number of elements from the yoga/mindfulness field and follow CASTEL standards that lessons be SAFE: sequenced, active, focused, and explicit (Payton et al., 2008). Each component is designed to explicitly teach and reinforce *Calm and Alert* concepts, offer children multisensory experiences in the concepts, and provide considerable practice of skills.

Class Components

Begin
Centering
Warm-up
Poses
Game
Rest
Centering/Close

Begin. Since the *Calm and Alert* class is distinctive in feel from other places a child might just have been, it is critical that the beginning of class be the time to establish a connection for children about the class and its relevance to the current setting. The immediate start of each class reminds children that the *Calm and Alert* class is a time to practice skills to help with learning and living using our body, mind, and breath. Quiet music can be put on at the start to allow for the sense that this learning has begun.

Begin

Setting tone, naming class concepts
Song/poem
Instruction/reminders about getting room ready for practice
Moving furniture
Getting a mat
Finding a place on the floor
Rolling out a mat
Sitting in the center of your mat, legs crossed, straight and tall

Song. The first part of "begin" is a song (also can be recited as a poem). Each topic has a corresponding song written to summarize the concepts for each lesson. The tune is familiar and repetitious (Frere Jacques) and the songs can be enhanced using American Sign Language (ASL) or other hand gestures for the adventurous. The songs have become a powerful mnemonic for children and adults, which have aided in the generalization and mastery of skills. Parents report children teaching family members the songs at appropriate times!

Calm and Alert Songs

All sung to the tune of "Frere Jacques."

Calm and Alert Song

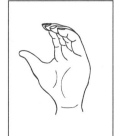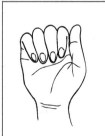

I am calm
I am calm
And alert
And alert
Every day at home
And every day at school
Calm, alert
Calm, alert

Calm Song

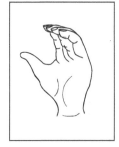

I am calm
I am calm
Quiet
Steady
No matter what happens
I can become
Quiet
Steady

Alert Song

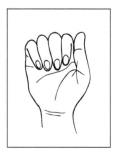

I am alert
I am alert
Awake
Ready to learn
Every day at home
Every day in school
Awake
Ready to learn

Respect Song

I am respectful
I am respectful
To others, myself
All things at school (or home)
Caring, gentle, serious
Caring, gentle, serious
Respectful
Respectful

Learning Time Song

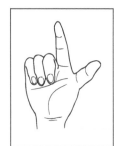

It is learning time
It is learning time
My number one job
My number one job
Listening and focus
Following directions
Learning time
Learning time

Transition Time Song

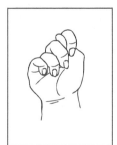

It's transition time
It's transition time
Time for change
Time for change
Mountain, cloud, and eagle
Steady, careful, focused
Transition time
Transition time

Social Time Song

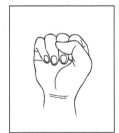

It is social time
It is social time
Time for friends (& family)
Time for friends (& family)
Eating, talking, playing
Safe and kind
Social time
Social time

Getting ourselves and the room ready. The second part of "begin" is getting ourselves and the room ready for our class/our practice. This comprehensively involves moving class desks/tables and chairs in order to clear a large area, and the use of small mats. For some of you, moving the furniture and using mats will seem more involved than you can imagine, which I respect and can be adapted. You also may encounter host teachers unwilling to have their rooms altered. But before closing the door of your mind, read further.

The power of the instruction and practice offered in the process of safely moving room furniture, carefully taking a mat from a bin or area, finding a space on the rug, rolling out a yoga mat, and finally sitting in the center of the mat ready for practice cannot be underestimated. Each step is explicitly taught and allows for rich learning in the area of respect, self-control, effortful control of movement, communication, consideration, and problem solving with others. Mastery of this process can take at least four lessons for many children, and will be addressed in the chapter on respect.

I have come to see that any skill deficit for a child in the area of self-regulation of learning-related social skills will be evident in their navigation of working with others to move furniture and the ability to practice steadily on a mat. I have witnessed many children start the year who roughly move the tables/chairs, grab and push at the mat bin, wander around unable to find a spot on the floor, and are unable to leave their mat flat on the floor or keep their body on the mat for class. These same children slowly, with instruction and practice, learn to be careful and gentle as they move tables with peers, calmly take a mat, roll it out, and sit waiting for practice. They also learn to take themselves and their practice seriously. Outside of class they then move more safely around the room, treat others and materials with more respect, and grow in self-awareness about their body and its movements.

Many of the class concepts could be taught with floor space but without mats, or simply as children stay at a desk, in a chair, or on a rug area. The sacrifice is the instruction concerning personal space as taught by staying on the mat, and the internalization of body control when a child can move freely. The class could also be taught in an alternative space outside a classroom (such as a gym), in a home or clinic—as discussed in following sections. I highly recommend, if possible, practicing in the actual location you want the skills to be utilized for better generalization.

Centering. Once children are on their mats, the core of the class unfolds. The beginning and end of the time on the mats is called "centering," a term used in yoga classes. This is when children are taught and practice erect posture, calm or alert breathing, how to tune into what they are thinking and feeling at that moment, and if needed, how to change their body, mind, or breath so they are available for the practice. This begins the explicit instruction in the calm and alert states.

A note on breath instruction: The intention of breathwork in *Calm and Alert* is to bring conscious awareness to the breath as a tool only, as a way of slightly altering a body/mind state if possible. It is not intensive, nor is it meditation. You will see throughout the book that breaths are only done consecutively in sets of two or three at most, there is never breath holding, and it is playful. At any time if a child reports feeling dizzy or uncomfortable, breathes rapidly for more than a few breathes, or holds their breath, the child should be cued to return to their normal breathing.

Centering

Sit in the middle of your mat cross-legged
Sit straight and tall
Learn, then practice breaths

There are **five calm breaths** and **four alert breaths** that can be taught:

Calm Breaths (5)

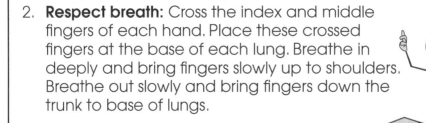

1. **Calm breath:** Sit up straight, place hands on belly, take a deep, slow breath in and out.

2. **Respect breath:** Cross the index and middle fingers of each hand. Place these crossed fingers at the base of each lung. Breathe in deeply and bring fingers slowly up to shoulders. Breathe out slowly and bring fingers down the trunk to base of lungs.

3. **Book breath:** Sit up straight and place index finger in the air. Breathe in to the count of three while moving finger horizontally to right. Breathe out to count of three, moving finger down toward floor. Breathe in to count of three, moving finger horizontally to left. Breathe out to count of three, moving finger up toward ceiling. This can also be done as an alert breath by making the same square shape with quick breaths in and out.

4. **M and M breath:** Sit up straight and place hand on chest. Take a deep breath in, close mouth, and make the "m" sound quietly as you exhale. Repeat; then ask: "Can you feel the sound making you calm?"

5. **Heart breath:** Sit up straight and place hands on top of head with curved fingers. Take a deep breath in and bring hands up in a curving motion like the top of a heart shape; breathe out and arch hands as they come down into the point of the heart. This can also be done as an alert breath with the same movements, but a quick breath in and out.

Alert Breaths (4)

(Caution: Use no more than three consecutive alert breaths.)

1. **Alert breath:** Place index and middle fingers on thumbs of each hand. Place these fingers alongside of eyes on each side. Take a quick breath in, open the eyes wide, and splay fingers away from thumb while bringing hands up toward ceiling. Bring hands back down with exhale.

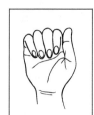

2. **Doggie breath:** Sit up straight with legs folded under, resting bottom on the feet. With "paws" in front of chest, breathe in two breaths in succession while wiggling nose; exhale a long, slow breath.

3. **Star breath:** Lace fingers in front of chest. Take a quick breath in and bring laced hands up to ceiling; exhale, and release hands out to sides and down while wiggling fingers (twinkling).

4. **"Yes" breath:** Make fists with hands and bring them to shoulders. Take a quick breath in and shoot hands up toward ceiling, opening the hands as arms straighten. Make fists again and bring them down toward shoulders while saying "yes" with a quick exhale.

Warm-ups. The warm-ups help prepare the body for the poses and other movements and are essential for safety. They employ the six movements of the spine and begin the instruction and practice in mindful movement.

Warm-ups

Six movements of the spine:
forward and back
side to side
twisting right and left

There are **four warm-ups** that can be used and all will be referenced in the ensuing chapters, depending on the chapter area and instruction needed:

1. Washing Machine

Sit up straight with your legs crossed. Think of some muddy thoughts you want to wash clean. Reach behind you and grab the muddy thoughts, then reach your arms up and over and pretend to put them in a washing machine in front of you. Close the lid. Now sit up straight, bring your arms close to your chest, and twist side to side slowly like a washing machine. Say "Ding" when it is done. Open the lid, reach in and pretend to shake out a shirt and name a clear thought. Reach behind you and put it in the dryer.

To do the dryer, sit up straight, breathe in and reach your arms up overhead, then place your right hand on the floor by your right side and reach your left arm overhead. Breathe in, center, then repeat this on the left side. Go back and forth a few times. Say "Ding" when the dryer is done. Reach into the dryer and pull out the clean shirt.

Breathe in and bring your hands up overhead; breathe out and bring your hands down to the sides of your body with a "yes breath."

2. Boat

Sit up straight with legs out in front of you. Prepare for your boat trip by reaching your arms up overhead and grabbing a life jacket; then pretend to put it on, keeping you safe. Twist to one side and grab a cushion, then twist to the other side and grab a blanket to keep you warm and comfortable in your boat. Reach behind you and grab a healthy snack. Grab your pretend oars in the air in front of your chest. Breathe in and sit up straight and slightly back; breathe out and bring the oars forward. Then repeat, moving forward and back a few times with the breath until you reach your destination.

3. Blast Off

Sit on your mat with your feet flat in front of you, knees bent. Place your hands behind your trunk: Feel steady here. Breathe out and slowly bring your knees down to the right. Breathe in and bring your knees back up. Now breathe out and bring your knees over to the left. Go back and forth two times. This movement will be the countdown for the blast off—starting with ten and knees to right, nine with knees to left, back and forth slowly until zero.

For blast off: Knees stay to the right as you push up onto your knees with your right hand near your right hip for support, and your left hand swinging up and over to the right. Then slowly come down and swing your knees to left for blast off on the left side. Then repeat on the other side: Keep your knees to the left as you push up onto your knees, your left hand near your hip for support, your right arm swinging up and over to the left.

4. Making Cookies

Sit up straight and tall on your mat with your legs out in front of you. Open your legs out so they form a "V." Pretend there is a bowl between your legs and we are ready to make cookies for our friends. Reach up with your right hand and grab an ingredient (flour) and put it in the bowl. Reach up with your left hand and grab another ingredient (oatmeal). Reach behind for butter on one side, then reach behind on the other side for honey, eggs, raisins, or other ingredients of your choosing and place them in bowl.

Pretend to mix the dough by making a big circle with your hands one way, then the other. Put out one forearm and imagine that this is our cookie sheet. With the other hand, pretend to scoop dough up and onto the sheet.

To bake, pretend to open the oven and place the cookies in. While you are waiting for them to bake, sing/recite a *Calm and Alert* song. When it is done say "Ding," take out the cookies, take a big breath in and blow on them to cool them. Then share your cookies with a friend. Smile.

Poses and flows. The *poses/movements* explicitly teach and require practice in: respect for the body, others and materials; mindful, careful movement; self-control; focus; positive attitudes toward the expectations. The *flows* offer a series of poses or movements that are related, which helps creates a body mnemonic for children. Many of the poses originating in the yoga tradition are renamed to enhance fun, decrease controversy, and enhance the themes. For example, the "half moon" is called the "pencil," the "child" is called the "puddle," and squats are called "calm frog" but are identical physically. The poses and flows will be referenced throughout the ensuing chapters, but can be used flexibly. Yoga figures are provided for visuals.

Poses

10 basic poses
5 flows

Calm and Alert Poses

Sitting mountain (three variations):

1. Sitting with legs folded under you, bottom resting on the "pillow of your feet," spine straight.

2. Sitting cross-legged on the floor, spine straight.

3. Sitting up straight in a chair with feet flat on floor, bottom on chair, hands resting on lap.

   Take a deep breath here. Bring attention to the "sitting bones": The two bones at the bottom of your bottom that rest on the floor or chair, keeping you grounded and steady.

Standing mountain: Standing with feet flat on floor, hip distance apart or together, spine straight, arms resting at sides. Can also be done with arms raised. Take a calm breath in and out while standing and "feel your mountain."

Cloud: Standing straight with arms wrapped around your upper chest in a self-hug, hands holding shoulders. Can be taught by starting with arms outstretched in a "T" position, then wrapping them across the body.

Rain: Stand in mountain, arms raised. Wiggle your fingers and imagine they are raindrops. Slowly bring wiggling fingers down your body—head, trunk, legs —then fold into the puddle.

Puddle (also known as "child's" pose): Start in sitting mountain; then fold trunk of body slowly over thighs, forehead touches floor, arms resting by side. Deep breathing here.

Frog: Squat with feet flat (or what is possible), knees wide, arms in between legs, hands touching floor.

Calm frog: Be as steady as possible, not moving, deep breaths.

Alert frog: Hop up with a quick breath in, down with a quick breath out.

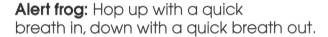

Warrior: Start in mountain. Tap on one leg and step it forward without strain; bend knee. Other leg is straight behind. Raise arms, look forward, deep breath.

Tree: Start in mountain. Tap on leg and put all weight on this leg. Point opposite toe and rest it next to standing leg on floor. Turn knee of pointed toe foot out to side. If steady here, try raising the bent knee leg up and rest foot on calf or thigh (not knee). If unsteady, bring foot down to floor. Repeat on other side.

Star: Starting in mountain, place hands on hips and hop legs out to a "V," keeping stance steady and feet on mat. Pause and feel steadiness. Now bring hands out to a "T" position. Twinkle by wiggling fingers, circling wrists, or making fists then quickly shooting fingers outward.

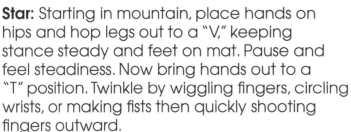

Variations: Hands overhead, bend forward and touch ground.

Eagle: Start with arms in cloud, feet together and knees bent—called perching eagle in flow.

Calm and Alert Pose Flows
School Tools

Calm pencil: Start in standing mountain. Inhale, arms up overhead bringing hands together into a point like a pencil. Remain steady.

Alert pencil: Breathe in, stay straight; exhale, bend right; inhale, center; exhale, bend left—a pencil writing.

Calm crayon: Like pencil above except pointed hands rest on top of head, elbows bent.

Alert crayon: Like alert pencil—moving side to side with breath; imagine coloring.

Calm marker: Start in standing mountain. Bring elbows close into sides, forearms folded to chest, thumbs touching shoulders. Remain steady; imagine being a marker with the cap on.

Alert marker: With an alert breath in, pop cap off by bringing arms quickly to ceiling; exhale, pop cap back on by bringing them down to calm position.

Calm scissors: Start in standing mountain. Inhale, raise arms overhead and cross hands so backs of hands are touching. Remain steady; imagine being a scissors resting.

Alert scissors: Alert breath in, arms come out wide in a "V" shape; exhale, bring arms back to center and clap hands—scissors cutting.

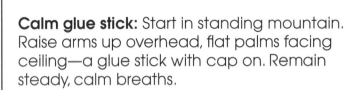

Calm glue stick: Start in standing mountain. Raise arms up overhead, flat palms facing ceiling—a glue stick with cap on. Remain steady, calm breaths.

Alert glue stick: Keeping steady with feet unmoving, breathe in and rotate just the trunk to right in a circle, imagining gluing the ceiling; exhale while finishing circle. Go the other way with next breath, staying as straight as possible.

Dogs

Calm sitting dog: Exactly like sitting mountain—legs folded under with bottom resting on feet, sitting straight on floor.

Calm standing dog (sometimes known as "table"): Come to hands and knees with hands under shoulders, knees under feet, straight back.

Puppy dog: Come into puddle (child's pose) but keep arms outstretched in front.

Arching/bowing dog: From calm standing dog, breathe out and arch the back, breathe in and bow the back.

Tail-wagging dog: Starting on hands and knees, imagine you have a tail. Breathe in, center, then curve to the right as you exhale and look for your tail. Breathe in, back to center; breathe out, curve to left. Go back and forth steadily, "not too fast, not too slow."

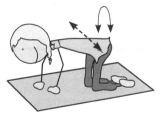

Twisty dog (also known as "thread the needle"):
Start on hands and knees. Lift up right hand
toward ceiling with a breath in; breathe out
and bring right hand down, under torso and
behind the left arm. Bottom stays in air,
knees firm on ground, right shoulder rests on
mat. Repeat on other side.

Up dog: Start on hands and knees, bring
hands a few inches toward the front
of mat. Breathe in, arch back so that
the face is turned up to ceiling, front
of legs flat on mat and the entire
body is one long arch upward.

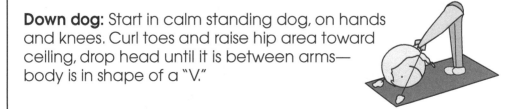

Down dog: Start in calm standing dog, on hands
and knees. Curl toes and raise hip area toward
ceiling, drop head until it is between arms—
body is in shape of a "V."

Resting dog: Lay on back, legs outstretched, arms at sides,
relaxed.

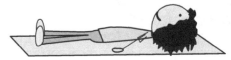

Frozen dog: From resting dog, bring straight arms and straight
legs toward ceiling and be frozen. Back is flat.

Happy dog (also known as "happy baby"): Lay on back in resting dog. Hug knees to chest, arms wrapped around legs. Grab outer edge of right foot with right hand, left foot with left hand. With back flat, spread feet out and up toward ceiling and rock back and forth.

Weather

Wind: Start in standing mountain, keeping feet firmly planted on ground. Lift arms into a "T" and sway upper arms and torso back and forth while making a windy sound with mouth. Used to illustrate the opposite of steady.

Rain: Stand in mountain, arms raised. Wiggle your fingers and image they are raindrops. Slowly bring wiggling fingers down your body—head, trunk, legs—then fold into the puddle.

Puddle (also known as "child's" pose): Start in sitting mountain; then fold trunk of body slowly over thighs, forehead touches floor, arms resting by side. Deep breathing here.

Frogs

Calm frog: Squat with feet flat (or what is possible), knees wide, arms in between legs, hands touching floor. Be steady and quiet as possible, not moving, deep breaths.

Alert frog: From calm frog, hop up with a quick breath in, down with a quick breath out. Try to hop without falling and land in the same spot you started on.

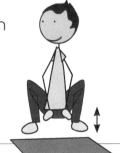

Tree climber: From calm frog, bring hands in front and in slow motion pretend to climb a tree, one hand moving on top of the other as you climb.

Tree: Start in mountain. Tap on leg and put all weight on this leg. Point opposite toe and rest it next to standing leg on floor. Turn knee of pointed toe foot out to side. If steady here, try raising the bent knee leg up and rest foot on calf or thigh (not knee). If unsteady, bring foot down to floor. Repeat on other side.

Eagle

Baby eagle: Squat with knees together, hands resting on mat on each side. Breathe.

Eagle stretching wings: From baby eagle, slowly bring arms out to sides as wings. As you breathe in, slowly come to standing position and bring arms up overhead until wrists touch. With the exhale, bring arms back to sides.

Perching eagle: Tuck hands into arm pits, elbows bent and tucked close to sides, knees slightly bent. Look from one side to the other.

Flapping eagle: Starting in mountain, bring arms out wide and up with an in-breath, down with an out-breath. Repeat slowly with calm breaths or quickly with alert breaths, a few at a time only.

Soaring eagle: Starting in mountain, bring arms out to a "T" position. With torso remaining straight, breathe in and center; as you breathe out, tilt torso to right. Repeat on other side, rhythmically going back and forth.

Hunting eagle: Starting in perching eagle, look down in front of toes and image there is a mouse you want to catch. Breathe in and bring arms up and overhead until wrists touch, then swoop down steadily and grab your mouse; return to standing and gobble it up!

The adult teacher, whenever comfortable, should show students the correct way to move and pose, and give feedback, including verbal corrections. To ensure physical and emotional safety, physical assists are not recommended in a school setting (Childress & Cohen-Harper, 2015), but in other settings discretion can be used. This helps students develop self-awareness of their bodies. After poses have been taught, children can become teachers and lead the class or teach their families quite skillfully.

Games. The games offer children a time of freer movement to practice the skills taught in the previous parts of class. There are four basic games offered:

- Stop
- Mountain/Cloud
- Touch One
- Switcheroo

Each game requires students to practice calm and alert states, safety in movement, self-control, and having fun without losing steadiness. There is explicit instruction given about: respectful walking and other movements, respectful body space and contact with others when appropriate, stopping your body on command, and smiling and having fun without dysregulation. Games always end with children returning to a mat (or space), standing in the center of their mats, and breathing. In each chapter, one of these games will be taught/referenced, some with variations based on the instruction of the chapter area. All the games are useful and can be selected flexibly.

Stop

Have child/children stand like a mountain in the middle of the mat or space. Put on some lively music (or simply say "go") and ask them to move in some way: hopping, skipping, galloping. These movements can be done on or off the mats or space.

Stop the music (or say "stop") and have child/children freeze or stop their bodies completely. Play music again with a direction for a movement, then stop music at random. Do as many times as you wish, with clear instruction that your body is safe and in control and it is fun to play a game when everyone is in control.

Mountain/Cloud

Have child/children stand like a mountain in the middle of the mat or space. After teaching "mountain" and "cloud" (standing, hugging arms around yourself and walking slowly and respectfully like a floating cloud), tell children you will now play the mountain/cloud game. Whenever you say "mountain" the children are to stand like a mountain wherever they are. Whenever you say "cloud" they are to float around the room. You can leave many seconds or just a few between words. You can add other poses as children become adept.

Touch One

Have child/children stand like a mountain in the middle of the mat or space. Put on lively music and give an instruction to move: hopping, skipping, or galloping (pick one). When the music stops, children freeze. You then say, "Touch one_____ (name a body part—pinky finger, toe) to someone else's _____ (same body part)." Say: "If you feel respected, smile at the person you are touching." In a school setting, it is best to use "elbow" and "shoulder" to help instruct these are the safest, most respectful ways to touch someone. Emphasize respectful touching and being in control.

Switcheroo

Have child/children stand like a mountain in the middle of the mat or space. Mention that the name of the game ("switcheroo") is a funny word for "change." Put on lively music and give instruction to move: hopping, skipping, or galloping (pick one). When the music stops, children freeze. You say, "Switcheroo _____ (1,2,3,4,5)" and children stand like mountains on a mat with that many people. Play music again and start a new round, each time giving a new number to the switcheroo. With much practice, you can put a blanket down and have a class of 25 students fit on one space.

Rest. The rest component of class has provided rich instruction for children in these areas: becoming calm after activity, learning to be and feel still, recognizing the feeling of relaxation, respecting the body's need for rest after exertion, and using stories and imagery for comfort. This has required an astounding amount of explicit instruction and practice for mastery, and has been the most beloved part of the class for children.

Rest

Body still, mind quiet
Finding a quiet, steady place inside
Picturing places of beauty and peace:
Mountain, garden, ocean, cozy house, night sky

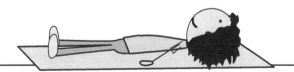

The rest component actually begins at the end of each game. Once children are standing back on their mats or space, they transition down to the ground using the "rain" which then becomes a "puddle." Children are encouraged to breathe and be aware that it is time for the body to become calm for rest. Then they roll on their backs and lay still with hands at their sides. When resting is first being taught in a group or individually, I expect children to simply lay on their backs, in order to ensure they begin to find within them a sense of "quiet, steady." As this becomes comfortably established, I allow them to "find what is most comfortable" as a way to rest, and children can lay on their sides, belly or back.

I often use a variety of music during class (calm music for warm-ups, poses, and rest; energizing music for games) and always use either quiet, instrumental music or silence during this component. The explicit instruction is to "be still" which means not moving. Being still is a skill that takes some children many lessons to understand, feel in their body, and master. For some children with special needs, just finding moments of stillness is important.

Once the room is quiet, I tell the students a relaxing story, developing their ability to use visualization as a tool for self-soothing—a common tool in the yoga and mindfulness fields. Each story starts by asking children to picture the sun and sky, and a big field; that they walk, skip, run, or hop down a path and by a steady stream to reach a peaceful place such as a mountain, a garden, an ocean, a cozy house, or star-studded night sky. Children are taught to use the imagery to come to know a quiet, steady place inside themselves that can be a soothing resource in times of need, which fosters resilience. The stories always end with children imagining leaving this quiet place, walking back through the field to their present setting, knowing they can always return.

Rest Time Script

"Lay on your back and become still on your mat by using your deep, calm breaths. Notice your feet, legs, torso, arms, hands, neck, and head and become still. This is how we rest our bodies.

Now we will rest our minds and heart with a story:

Picture a beautiful blue sky and the sun shining down on you. Imagine a big field and see yourself walk, skip, run, or hop through the field. You hear, then see, a steady stream and walk beside it. The bubbling sounds seem to say 'lay all your cares in my waters' and you take any cares you have and imagine them washed away by the stream. You keep walking until you reach a _____ (mountain, garden, ocean, cozy house, night sky—pick one).

See yourself step into this place, and as you do feel any cares you may have leaving your mind or heart. Look around the _____ (mountain, garden, ocean, cozy house, night sky). Notice flowers, trees, sand, ocean, stars (guide them to picture whatever is beautiful about that particular place). Let the beauty and sounds remind you of a quiet, steady place you have inside you."

Pause here and allow silence for a few minutes.

"Now it is time to say goodbye to your beautiful place, but we never have to leave our quiet, steady place—it is always with you. Walk back through the field to _____ (their present setting). Turn on your side and pause there. Bring your knees into your chest, wrap your arms around your knees and give yourself a hug. Now push yourself up to sitting."

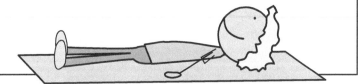

Centering/Close. After turning onto their sides and pushing themselves up to sitting in an unhurried way, children learn to tune in to how they feel and chose a calm or alert breath to help them be ready for the following transitions: rolling up and putting away their mats, returning the room to its original state, and preparing for the next time of the day or the next expectation.

Centering at End

Calm and alert states are noticed
Attention to how you feel
Choose a calm or alert breath to help you
Mats rolled up and put away
Room is restored
Song sung/recited one final time

Calm and Alert Planner

Materials:

- Chime
- Hoberman sphere
- Mind, body, breath icons
- Picture of spine
- Pictures of six basic feelings: happy, sad, scared, angry, surprised, disgusted
- Paint chip
- Jar of clear water; jar of mud
- On/off switch

Begin:

Calm and Alert songs:
Respect song
Calm song
Alert song
Learning Time song
Transition Time song
Social Time song

Centering:

Calm Breaths
Calm breath
Respect breath
M and M breath
Book breath
Heart breath

Alert Breaths
Alert breath
Doggie breath
Star breath
Yes breath

Warm-ups:

Washing Machine
Boat
Blast Off
Making Cookies

Poses:

Standing mountain
Sitting mountain
Cloud
Rain
Puddle
Frog
Warrior
Tree
Star
Eagle

Pose Flows:
School Tools flow
Weather flow
Dog flow
Eagle flow
Frog flow

Games:

Stop
Mountain/Cloud
Touch One
Switcheroo

Rest (stories):

Mountain
Garden
Ocean
Cozy House
Night Sky

Lesson 1: Calm and Alert Basics

Body   Mind   Breath

Begin. Have children at their seats (table or floor). Show them the three icons and tell them we will be learning more about how to use these to help us learn. Say, "We will learn a chant at the beginning of class, do some movements, then learn a song at the end of class." While they are still sitting, have them push back their chairs (if in chairs) and teach them this chant:

The Body, Mind, Breath Chant

My body is my helper when it's in control.

My mind is my helper when it's ready to learn.

My breath is my helper when it's calm and alert.

- As they chant the first line (they can echo you), have them tap their knees.

- As they chant the second line, have them tap their heads.

- As they chant the third line, have them tap their torso where the lungs abide.

Centering. Have children stand up or walk to a rug area and form a circle, then sit on the rug. Ask them to sit up straight, which can be illustrated by rolling the shoulders up, back, and down and tucking the chin. Then ask students to first notice their breathing, then put their hands on their bellies and take a slow, deep breath. Say, "This is the calm breath."

Calm breath: Sit up straight, take a deep breath in and out.

Warm-up. "Sit and stand like a mountain" instruction begins here. The mountain is the foundation of all body positions in class and must be explicitly taught this first class in this warm-up component. Sitting like a mountain requires you fold your calves and feet under you and sit with your spine straight. Be sure your feet are in a "V" shape and create a hollow or "pillow" for your bottom. Recite the body portion of the chant again in this position. Now have children stand like a mountain: feet hip distance apart (about four inches), straight and tall, hands at their sides, feeling steady like a rock. You can repeat the body portion chant again, faster or slower, with clapping or snapping. Have students take a breath in and raise their arms overhead for the "full" mountain pose (call it the tallest mountain in the world), then exhale and bring arms down to their sides.

Pose/Game. Pose and game is combined in this first lesson. While children are still standing, begin the explicit instruction of body, mind, and breath.

Explicit instruction about the body. Have students stay standing in a circle. Hold up the body icon and ask, "Where is your body?" Then wait for responses. Then say, "That is a funny kind of question, isn't it? Your body is everywhere you touch." Have children tap different parts of their bodies as you name them. To enhance beginning awareness of self-control, as they move ask, "Are you in control or out of control right now?" and point out children who are being mindful in their movements.

Explicit instruction about the mind. Remain standing or have children sit like a mountain. Hold up the mind icon and ask, "Where is your mind? Do you know another name for mind?" Point to the icon and then your head. Recite the mind portion of the chant while tapping your head and have them repeat it. Tell students our minds are constantly making thoughts (words) and images (pictures), some of which can help us or get in our way. When you are "ready" or "ready to learn" your thoughts and pictures are clear, positive, and helping you. Ask, "Who can name a clear, positive thought?" (I like this; I am happy; I can do it; I will try.)

Explicit instruction about the breath. Sitting or standing, ask students what body part helps them breathe. Show them the icon of the lungs and have them gently pat with two hands the place where the lungs reside, modeling one hand on one side, one on the other. Recite the breath portion of the chant while patting the chest, and have the children repeat. Explain how breathing can be shallow (illustrate a small breath) or deep (illustrate by counting in four and out four). You can use a balloon to show that the lungs are like a balloon—blow it up and release. When we say our breath helps us when it is calm or alert, it is a way we can use our breath on purpose to help us. If available, use a Hoberman sphere, which I call a "breathing ball." A calm breath is a slow, deep breath in and out. As you breathe in, expand the ball; as you breathe out, collapse the ball. An alert breath is quick in, quick out. Have them do two and notice how it feels, and illustrate by having the sphere go in and out quickly. Alert breaths wake us up; they give oxygen to the brain. Wrap up by saying we can choose calm breaths when we need to calm down and alert breaths when we need to wake up.

Rest. If children are still standing, have them stand like a mountain, breathe in and put their hands overhead. Create "rain" by wiggling  fingers and then gently tapping the body as your arms and whole body comes down into sitting mountain. If students are sitting cross-legged, just transition them to sitting mountain. From sitting mountain, breathe in, then exhale into puddle by folding the torso over the thighs, resting the forehead on floor. Have them stay here for a few deep breaths. Say, "Can you feel your body beginning to relax and be calm?" Now have them breathe in and come back up to sitting mountain, eyes open. Smile.

Centering/Close. Review concepts, use chant once more with a challenge to do it without your help, or assign a child to be a "teacher/leader." Challenge children to stand like a mountain and then walk like a mountain back to their seats. When they are back at their seats, introduce the *Calm and Alert* song:

Calm and Alert Song

I am calm
I am calm
And alert
And alert
Every day at home
And every day in school
Calm, alert
Calm, alert

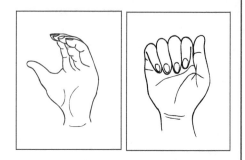

Every *Calm and Alert* song is sung to the familiar tune of "Frere Jacques." Words can be adapted for a particular setting and ASL signs (see an ASL dictionary) can be used as hand movements while you sing. Practice the chant, song, breaths, and poses daily if possible after this lesson.

At the close of this lesson, if you plan to use mats in the future, have a rolled-up mat with you and show it to the children, saying, "Next time I come, we will each get a mat to learn from."

Calm and Alert Lesson: The Basics

Lesson 1

Grade/Group_____   Date_____

Materials needed:
Body, mind, breath icons on poster or blocks
Rolled-up mat
Balloon

Lesson

Begin:
Chant/poem: Body, mind, breath chant

My **body** is my helper when it's in control.

My **mind** is my helper when it's ready to learn.

My **breath** is my helper when it's calm and alert.

Centering:
The calm breath

Warm-up:
Standing mountain
Sitting mountain
Rain
Puddle

Poses/Game:
Body, mind, breath chant/instruction
Standing or sitting mountain

Rest:
Puddle

Centering/Close:
The calm breath
Calm and Alert song

Teaching and Using Calm and Alert in Other Settings

The basic Calm and Alert concepts and components can be taught explicitly in an office, small group session, or a yoga studio. If possible, follow the guidelines under "Teaching Calm and Alert as a Class" with modifications for time and the skill level of the child/children you are serving, offered here.

The Calm and Alert Basics

Body, mind, breath concepts, in chant
The steadiness of the mountain
The calm of the puddle
The calm breath
Calm and Alert song

Whatever your setting, the class components and structure create a flow for a session and can offer regularity for later instruction of skills. You can do just a small amount of teaching in each component, shortening the time, the number of movements, or teaching points. The material in this "basics" lesson can and should be done over multiple sessions with sensitivity to your population until you feel the children have a solid foundation in the chant and the body, mind, breath concepts; the flow of the lesson components; taking conscious breaths; the steadiness expected in the sitting and standing mountain; the puddle; the song (if that is a priority).

If utilizing all the components is too much due to cognitive delays, attention issues, inflexibility, or other special issues, prioritize teaching the sitting and standing mountain, the puddle, and the calm breath. Then teach the chant one line at a time each week, or the song over time. The chant and song have been very popular with my special needs students and are a powerful mnemonic.

Use small mats. Although the mats are not yet rolled out in Lesson 1, I recommend introducing the presence of a mat and the hope that it can be used as soon as you can with individual children or small groups. The mats I use are four feet long, which I use for children aged five to eight; but depending on your space, larger or smaller mats can be used. As noted earlier, the mats offer so much opportunity for instruction, particularly for children who are hyperactive, have little body awareness, and need a lot of practice becoming regulated.

Start your instruction by showing a child the rolled-up mat and have them hold it, then roll out the mat and teach them to sit in the middle of their mat "like a mountain." See the chapter on Respect for more instruction about the mats, particularly if you are using them with small groups.

Use visuals and a chime. The body, mind, and breath icons (Appendix 2) will be a useful visual as you continue to build the *Calm and Alert* skills, particularly with visual learners. Although not utilized in this first lesson, consider purchasing some kind of chime (zen chime is recommended in the materials list) that has a sound that echoes for at least 20 seconds. You can introduce it now as you begin, by ringing it and asking the children to "just listen as long as you can" or "be a mountain as long as the sound lasts." It can help some children feel successful for a short period with a clear beginning and ending. Experiment with using visuals, the chime, the chant, the song, and movements flexibly to see which modality best reaches a particular child, keeping the basics you want to teach as your beacon.

Expect it to feel very new. These practices and concepts are very new for many adults and children, particularly if you are a beginner to such practices and if you are helping a child whose preferences are unusual. Expect it to feel awkward and accept mistakes (your own and the children's) with forgiveness. Things will become smoother as you practice, or you may find it is not a perfect match for you or the child you are helping.

Modifying the Class Elements

Begin. If time or attention spans are limited and the chant would be too much to introduce, show the children the body, mind, breath icons and have them just quickly touch a place on their body, their brain, and their lungs. Or just teach one component per session, starting with the body and that line from the chant over multiple sessions. Show them a mat if you plan to use them in the future, and roll it out to build excitement.

Body   Mind   Breath

Centering. Ring your chime. Have the children put their hand on their lung area and take a deep breath. This will plant a seed of awareness about the chime and the breath and establish that you will always ask them to do so when you begin. Use of the balloon for instruction or the breathing ball (Hoberman sphere) in the beginning can offer engagement for some, but can be overly exciting for others.

Warm-up. If at all possible, teach the sitting and standing mountains, as explained in the previous section. If only one can be taught, start with the sitting mountain. Praise every detail: folding the legs under, sitting still for even a few seconds, being steady for even a few seconds.

Poses/Game. Modify, if needed, the explicit instruction about the mind, body, and breath, but touch on each using the icons, if possible. If not, start with just the body. Bring awareness to each part of the body by touching each lightly. Children can be sitting or standing.

Rest. Teaching the puddle this first time has many advantages. It is a pose that children can choose to use in many settings when they feel out of control and need to reset themselves, and it establishes the importance of rest after learning. If time is short, at least model the puddle yourself and invite the children to try it for a few seconds.

Centering/Close. Ring your chime. Have children again put a hand on their lung area and take one or multiple deep breaths. Teach the *Calm and Alert* song if it is not too much. Bring the children's awareness to the transition to come, from this practice to whatever is next for them. Have a rolled-up mat with you, and say, "Next time, we will learn more about having a mat" if you plan to use one in the future.

Teaching and Using Calm and Alert at Home

Many modern families struggle with the demands of busy schedules, high expectations for achievement, and the constant stimulation the culture offers children. Despite this trend, you can expect your typically developing or special needs child to learn the *Calm and Alert* concepts and states, and it will make your home life easier and more enjoyable. With your guidance, your child can be taught to become calm if over-excited, remain alert even when fatigued, and sustain both states when needed.

The Calm and Alert Basics at Home

Calm and alert breaths
The sitting and standing mountain
The puddle

Read "Basic Calm and Alert Concepts." If at all possible, read the basic calm and alert concepts section of this chapter; have the body, mind, breath icons in your home; and see if your child is comfortable learning the chant. It will establish a foundational shared vocabulary for all the members of your family that can be used anywhere.

For example, imagine your family at a restaurant and it is almost time to leave. Your child is becoming restless, wiggly, and loud. With the bedrock of your above practice, you could say, "We are about to leave the restaurant and go home. Your body needs to be your helper by being in control. Let's pick a clear thought about going home and all take a deep breath to become calm."

Calm and Alert Breaths. If you are committed to bringing the calm and alert skills into your home, seriously consider purchasing a Hoberman expanding mini sphere to encourage calm and alert breaths and a chime or bell to quickly remind your child of these states and to get their attention for breathing.

A Hoberman sphere is a toy many children are familiar with, and it can playfully be used to teach and encourage breathwork. For a calm breath: Expand it slowly as your child inhales; collapse it slowly as your child exhales. For an alert breath: Expand it quickly as your child inhales; collapse it quickly as your child exhales. A balloon, as suggested in the class section, can also be used.

Select a bell or chime whose sounds echoes for at least 10 or 20 seconds (zen chime recommended). Introduce it to your family as a special chime that will help everyone to pause and take a minute to become calm and alert. Practice by having everyone stop what they are doing, ring the chime, and ask everyone to listen attentively until they cannot hear the sound anymore. If you want further practice, ask your child to then take three or more deep breaths, and ring the chime once more or multiple times. Imagine ringing the chime before dinner, when you need the family to focus before a transition to an outing, or before bed.

Mountain and Puddle Poses. Throughout this book you will hear about many poses, but the two essential poses for your home are mountain and puddle.

Sitting and standing mountain. Your child can sit like a mountain by becoming aware of the two "sitting bones" at the bottom of their bottom (more instruction in the Respect chapter), and feel them firmly planted on the earth while sitting cross-legged on the floor or in a chair. Back should be straight and body should be still. They can also fold their legs under them so the sitting bones are on the heels and the calves are touching the back of the thighs, if this is comfortable. Standing like a mountain requires standing straight and tall with feet hip distance apart and not moving. With practice, you can say to a wiggly child "be a mountain," and you will see them become steady.

Puddle. The puddle is called the "child's" pose in the yoga tradition, but this name brings the imagery of still water to help teach this resting state. From the sitting mountain with legs folded under as described above, have your child take a deep breath in and fold their trunk of the body over the thighs and place the arms down to the sides. Have them breathe deeply for a few breaths, and teach your child they have a quiet, steady place inside them. You can place your hand on the back for an added comfort. For a child who struggles to self-soothe, the puddle is an ideal tool.

You can cue your child to use these poses in many settings. While waiting in line for a movie, say, "Stand like a mountain;" after company leaves when your child is wound up, say, "Become a puddle."

Chapter TWO
Respect

### Respect Song	

Respect Song

I am respectful
I am respectful
To others, myself
All things at school (or home)
Caring, gentle, serious
Caring, gentle, serious
Respectful, respectful

Respect, as a word and concept for young people, is at risk today. As a word it is sometimes under- and overused, and as a concept it is difficult to define, especially for children. Culturally, we expect young people to be respectful, notice and become offended when they are not, and sometimes discipline them for its lack. Yet our children see disrespect everywhere: news and social media, screen entertainments, community events, sports, and politics, including admired heroes and heroines who are revealed to be other than heroic. This creates a great deal of confusion and a consequential, noticeable lack of skill in areas of respect for many.

The reality for children is that understanding and practicing respect requires thousands of hours of role modeling by adults in their life, limit setting when disrespectful, and explicit explanations and teaching about how to practice. Whether we are helping a child who has had these thousands of hours or none, they need us to hold this beacon of humanity for them while they learn. Without an expectation of respect, a relationship with a child or children tends to be difficult, as they can be demanding, hurt people and things without apology, or treat the task or event at hand as unimportant. If not remedied, it can be very impairing. Every person in every relationship deserves respect, especially the adults in children's lives who do so much to care for them. It is a very beautiful, very worthy concept to teach.

The fruit of my years of inquiry concerning what respect is, and how to teach it to young people, has resulted in the *Calm and Alert* definition, "caring, gentle, and serious." This grew after careful observation of respect/disrespect in children, particularly by age five when they begin formal schooling. Many children were making *caring* mistakes by hurting people with words and actions and careless treatment of things resulting in breakage and harm. *Gentle* mistakes were happening as children treated others and things roughly, lacked spontaneity in helping when a need arose, or exhibited mean behavior. Mistakes through a lack of *seriousness* were happening with more children being exceptionally silly, appearing unmotivated to learn a task, or belittling people, things, or tasks.

The dictionary definition most closely aligned would be "due regard for the feelings, wishes, or rights of others," and I would add "things of this world." **What the *Calm and Alert* definition offers are three aspects of respect that can be concretely taught, practiced, and understood.** Through the explicit instruction outlined in this chapter, there has been noticeable improvement in all of these areas of concern, and the children show enthusiasm and satisfaction in learning and practicing the skills. Another benefit is the affirmation and support the instruction offers children who already practice respect daily, because it gives the concept the validation of attention and instruction.

Ultimately, the primary, most powerful tool you have is your own offering of respect in the relationship between you and a child (or group of children), and the way you treat everything: your caring toward the children, your gentleness with the mats and space, and your seriousness about the importance of the teaching. This foundational reverence for and confidence in respect in *Calm and Alert* grows out of the yoga/mindfulness tradition with its emphasis on careful tending of the body, mind, and breath which then flowers into careful tending of other people and things around you.

I always say, then teach the children to respond, "I respect you" at the end of each class/session, as an explicit way to begin the teaching, and am very earnest.

Although awkward and possibly not genuine for them at first, over weeks of practice it becomes a favorite phrase, repeated at various times of the day spontaneously to myself and others. Over the years, it has become something the adults in my community say to one another as well.

Respect Concepts

Respect = caring, gentle, serious

Caring = you never harm yourself, others or things
Gentle = careful, helpful, and kind
Serious = this matters

I treat myself, others, and all things with respect at all times.

Teaching Respect as a Class

Begin
Centering
Warm-up
Poses
Game
Rest
Centering/Close

Lesson 2: I Am Respectful

Begin. Have the body, mind, breath icons visible as you begin the lesson. Remind the children of your last lesson/teaching, and even quickly do the chant if time allows.

With the children at their tables, desks, or sitting on a rug, introduce the class concept by saying, "Today we are going to learn about respect and being respectful. We will begin by learning the 'Chime Practice.'" Show the children your zen or other chime, and ask them to "listen as long as they can" as you ring it the first time. Notice how seriously they take the challenge. Then ask them to put their hands on their bellies and take a calm breath as they did last time. You can ask them to take one to five breaths here, then ring the chime again and listen as long as they can. End this portion by saying that you will always start with the chime practice as a sign of respect for your practice together.

Chime Practice

Ring chime, listen as long as you can
Lead children in 3–5 slow, deep breaths
Ring chime, listen as long as you can

Then teach the children the Respect song line by line, or chant it as a poem. I use my hands by incorporating ASL: index and middle fingers of both hands crossed (letter R) and held up as you sing/say "I am respectful," an open palm gesture toward "others," then hand on your chest when you sing "myself," finally scan the room with your crossed fingers when you sing "all things at school/home."

Respect Song

I am respectful
I am respectful
To others, myself
All things at school (or home)
Caring, gentle, serious
Caring, gentle, serious
Respectful, respectful

Next sit down yourself at a table or desk and explain how important it is that we treat everything with respect. Put your hand over your heart, have the children do the same, and say, "Respect starts here and feels good to practice." For children up to age seven or eight, you can have fun by pointing to the chairs and tables and have them echo: "I respect you chairs," then "I respect you tables;" while also asking, "How do chairs and tables help us?"

Now model being steady and careful as we move tables to get the room ready. Refer to the previous lesson in which we learned to stand like a mountain, and model this as you get up from your seat. Ask, "How am I a mountain?" Then model gently pushing in a chair and ask, "How am I gentle?" Have all the children (or one table at a time) stand like mountains and push in chairs gently. Establish this first time that children should always ask the question "Is it safe?" before moving the table with their peers and the answer should be "yes" before proceeding. Practice this. **Note that when everyone is serious, everything is safe.** Closely monitor how tables are being moved: Reinforce those being respectful, stop those moving too fast, etc. When inevitable problems arise, such as the accidental tipping of a chair, slow down and address it, modeling respect.

Have children this first time sit on the floor "like a mountain" (as learned in the last lesson) after moving the furniture. Take one small mat yourself out of the bin and place it, still tightly rolled, vertical between your two knees and hug it gently to your chest, all the while describing what you are doing. This is called "sitting like a little mountain with the mat between your legs." Model being steady, not squeezing, folding, or unraveling your mat. Say, "I am thinking, 'I respect you mat' as I hold it."

Then call four to five children at a time to get a mat and sit like a mountain with the mat between their legs in a row, facing you at the front of the room where you are placed for teaching. Have other children notice how they are being respectful with questions such as: "What do you see that is caring, gentle, serious?" Continue to call four to five children with the same attention until rows are established, about four feet apart to accommodate rolled out mats. As the teacher, you should look out and see a "mountain range" of children sitting in rows with mats between their legs, steady.

Next, model for the children turning their mats sideways in front of them without rolling them out. This pause allows you to explicitly teach appropriate boundaries with space, and that it is a sign of respect for self, others, and all things around you. Children's mats should not touch and they should look to see that they will have enough room to roll out their mat without touching others. Then give the direction to roll out mats, mentioning there might be problems to solve. These include mats touching, mats crooked, mats curling up. Smile and be light hearted, showing that "any problem can be solved calmly." Once mats are rolled out and flat, have children sit cross-legged in the middle of their mat.

This "begin" portion can take many weeks for mastery and it is worth taking as much time as needed to establish this level of respect for practice. If rushed, valuable instruction can be lost. It is a pleasure to see this portion of a lesson stabilize: smooth moving of tables, orderly getting of mats, fewer problems rolling mats out, pride as they sit in the middle of their mats.

Centering. Draw the class' attention to how they are sitting: legs crossed in the middle of their mat. Have them notice that the "middle" means there is room in front and behind, as well as on either side. With hands on their knees, have then rock back and forth and feel their "sitting bones," the two little bones at the bottom of their bottom. Then have then stop and feel the bones keeping them steady, like feet. If available, show them a picture of a spine and ask them to sit up straight. Say, "When we sit up straight and keep our sitting bones steady, we show respect for our bodies."

Have the children put up their respect signs used in the song and model putting the crossed fingers at the bottom of the lungs for the respect breath. Repeat two to three times. Point out how caring and gentle the breath is as it comes in and out of the body, keeping us alive every minute of every day.

Respect Breath

Cross the index and middle fingers of each hand. Place these fingers at the base of each lung. Breathe in deeply and bring fingers slowly up to shoulders. Breathe out slowly and bring fingers down trunk to base of lungs.

As you finish, have them tap their respect signs on the area of their heart and say, "Respect starts here, in our hearts."

Warm-up. Have everyone now come to sitting at the back of their mats with their legs out in front of them for a short body scan before the Boat warm-up. Say, "Let's get our bodies ready for a boat trip," and have them tap their feet, then legs, then trunk, then arms, clap hands, and tap head. With each body part say, "We are so lucky to have legs, arms, etc." You can even say, "I respect you legs, arms, etc." for fun. Also ask, "Are you showing respect for yourself and others by staying on your mat and touching your body gently?"

For this first Boat warm-up, you can teach it in its entirety as offered:

Boat

Sit up straight with legs out in front of you. Prepare for your boat trip by reaching your arms up overhead and grabbing a life jacket; then pretend to put it on, keeping you safe. Twist to one side and grab a cushion, then twist to the other side and grab a blanket to keep you warm and comfortable in your boat. Reach behind you and grab a healthy snack.

Grab your pretend oars in the air in front of your chest. Breathe in and sit up straight and slightly back; breathe out and bring the oars forward. Then repeat, moving forward and back a few times with the breath until you reach your destination.

Or you can keep it simpler and start by "grabbing oars" and slowly rowing back and forth. The emphasis should be that we show respect for ourselves and others when we move carefully and gently, not "too fast or too slow."

Poses. Ask the children to "get out of their boats" and sit like a mountain as they learned last time and model the pose. Bring their awareness to their sitting bones here. Hands on heart, have them notice their breath. Now count to three and ask them to stand like a mountain in the middle of their mats and draw their attention once again to what the middle looks like. When you are a mountain, you show respect for yourself, others, and all things, because you are steady and safe.

Sitting mountain (three variations):

1. Sitting with legs folded under you, bottom resting on the "pillow of your feet," spine straight.

2. Sitting cross-legged on the floor, spine straight.

3. Sitting up straight in a chair with feet flat on floor, bottom on chair, hands resting on lap.

   Take a deep breath here. Bring attention to the "sitting bones": the two bones at the bottom of your bottom that rest on the floor or chair, keeping you steady.

Standing mountain: Standing with feet flat on floor, hip distance apart or together, spine straight, arms resting on sides. Can also be done with arms raised. Take a calm breath while standing and "feel your mountain."

Now teach them this poem, by saying: "Stay standing like a mountain and get your clapping hands ready in front of your chest." For younger children, clap and say each line and have them repeat; for older children, say/clap in its entirety. Repeat, and in between repetitions have the children take a breath in and raise their hands overhead to be the "tallest mountain in the world."

Mountain Poem

I am a mountain
Steady and tall
Nothing
Can make me fall

If time allows, also consider having the children remain with their hands in the air and pretend to "be the wind" as a challenge to their steadiness. Make windy sounds and move your arms and yourself around the class saying, "Stay steady even as the wind comes by!" This begins the instruction about having fun without losing control.

Game. For this first time if teaching young children, play the Stop game on the mats only. Use the opportunity to instruct them about respecting space: Have them walk slowly around the periphery of their mat, then hop into the middle and be a mountain. Say, "When everyone respects space by being on their mat, no one has to worry about anything unsafe happening."

Stop

Have child/children stand like a mountain in the middle of the mat or space. Put on some lively music (or simply say "go") and ask them to move in some way: hopping, skipping, galloping. These movements can be done on or off the mats or space. Stop the music (or say "stop") and have child/children freeze or stop their bodies completely. Play music again with a direction for a movement, then stop music at random. Do as many times as you wish, with clear instruction that your body is safe and in control and it is fun to play a game when everyone is in control.

Rest. As the games ends, have children stand in the middle of their mats like a mountain. Remind them of the rain and puddle, then lead the group: breathing in, raising arms overhead, "finding their gentle rain" by wiggling their fingers and gently tapping their fingers down the body in slow motion until they then fold into a puddle. Model for them and mention that the puddle respects all the parts of our bodies, inside and out. Have them take a few calm breaths here, then dim the lights and have them roll onto their backs for rest time.

This first time, spend time explicitly instructing the children in "laying steady like a mountain" on their backs, with their entire body on the mat. Model by laying on your mat, then point out children who are practicing. Explicitly teach the concept of being still by saying, "Still means not moving," and draw their attention to each part of their bodies by saying, "Are your feet still? Are your legs still? If the answer is yes, stay still, if the answer is no, become still." Being still respects the body's need for rest.

Once everyone is practicing to the best of their abilities, begin the rest time story, this time visiting a mountain.

Rest Time Script: The Mountain

"Now that we are resting our bodies by being still, we will rest our hearts and minds with a rest time story.

Picture a beautiful blue sky and the sun shining down on you; feel the sun shining on a steady place inside you. Imagine a big field and see yourself walk, skip, run, or hop through the field. You hear, then see, a quiet, steady stream and walk beside it. The bubbling sounds seem to say 'lay all your cares in my waters.' You reach down and touch the water, and imagine them washed away by the stream. The stream takes you to the foot of a beautiful mountain.

Imagine sitting down by the stream and looking up at the mountain, noticing flowers, trees, birds—all keeping you company. Let the beauty remind you of a quiet, steady place you have inside you. Feel the strength of the mountain inside you."

Pause here and allow silence for a few minutes.

"Now it is time to say goodbye to the beautiful mountain, but we never have to leave our quiet, steady place—it is always with you. Walk back through the field to _____ (their present setting). Turn on your side and pause there. Bring your knees into your chest, wrap your arms around your knees and give yourself a hug. Feel proud that you have shown respect to yourself, others, and all things in our class. Now push yourself up to sitting."

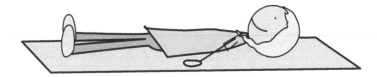

Centering/Close. Give the class a chance to slowly sit up and settle cross-legged on their mats. Some children may be reluctant to sit back up, say they are tired, or on occasion fall asleep, which is fine—simply repeat the expectation to sit up. Now return to the respect breath for three to five breaths. Quietly remind them that we learned this breath at the start of class and the breath is helping us remember all we have learned about respect.

This first time, explicitly teach how to roll up a mat and sit again "like a sitting mountain with the mat between your legs." Have the children watch as you come to the back of your mat, and sit steady as you begin. Talking through each step as you model, with the mat flat on the floor, curl up the mat tightly as you begin. With "eyes on your mat, hands never leaving the mat" press and roll, moving the body forward. Once the mat is "as tight as it can be," sit with it between the legs and model waiting. I have come to understand that this process of rolling up the mat carefully and becoming steady while waiting offers many children needed instruction in internal organization.

Once you see a "mountain range" of children, ask everyone: "Are you steady?" Tap children gently who look steady as a cue to stand like a mountain, holding their mats close to the body as they walk out to the bin or place for returning the mat. As they return after replacing their mat, have them stand by their table for others to arrive. The group around a table can then ask again "is it safe?" as they did at the beginning; and when safety is established, move the furniture gently back into place. Continue your instruction by asking: "Are you careful, are you gentle, are you serious?" Once furniture is back, have children sit like mountains in their seats.

If time allows, end the class by singing the Respect song once more. Put your hand on your heart and say to the class, "I respect you," as you bring your open hand out to the class. Teach them to respond by saying, "I respect you," to you.

Calm and Alert Lesson: I Am Respectful

Lesson 2

Grade/Group_____   Date_____

Materials needed:
Body, mind, breath icons
Chime
Picture of a spine
Mats in mat bin

Lesson

Begin:
Chime practice
Respect song

Centering:
The respect breath

Warm-up:
Boat

Poses:
Standing/sitting mountains with poem:
   I am a mountain
   Steady and tall
   Nothing
   Can make me fall
Rain
Puddle

Game:
Stop (have children stay on mats)

Rest:
First instruction in rest: mountain

Centering/Close:
Respect breath
Respect song

Teaching and Using Respect in Other Settings

The basic concepts and materials can be useful for small groups, special populations, and various spaces. (If you have not done so, read the previous section on "Teaching Respect as a Class" for many explicit details of instruction.) Offered here are the recommended essentials and modifications, including a reminder that you can shorten, combine, or break up all class elements, but use the previous template as your guide.

Recommended Essentials for Respect

Being a caring, gentle, and serious adult
Using the song/poem as a teaching tool
Chime practice
Body space and awareness instruction
Mountain, rain, and puddle poses

Your caring, gentleness, and seriousness with the children you serve is the most essential foundation for the instruction. This role modeling flows through everything you say and do as you focus on the other essentials.

Modifying Class Elements

Begin. The essentials as you begin are utilizing the space, the chime, and the song for your foundational instruction of respect.

Consideration for your available space is very important and can affect how you begin the teaching. Some of you may have a studio, office, or gym that offers an open space for the start of practice, and may or may not be using mats. You have many options:

- Have them stand in mountain as they arrive to the room, and establish your expectations for finding a space on the floor.
- Lay all the mats out (or small rugs or other visuals) before the children arrive and have them immediately "sit in the middle of their mats/rugs cross-legged."

• Have them assemble on the floor around you, sitting like a mountain, and begin the respect teaching before they get their mats by using the chime and singing the song.

As mentioned previously, this first class establishes the habits of respect, including an orderly and calm start to the practice, so take your time establishing the above.

Once the children are initially settled, offer the instruction on the chime practice and sing the song/chant. The teaching of the chime practice and song can be done over multiple sessions. Bring their awareness to the room and how it will be helping us practice. If sitting already on a mat/rug, have them notice their mats/rugs by feeling all the edges—if you are not using mats/rugs, have them outline a personal space around themselves in a wide circle on the floor with their hands and say: "We respect our space and the space of others." If you plan to have them retrieve a mat from a bin in the room, follow the guidelines for "begin" in the previous section.

Centering. The essentials of centering for the concept of respect are awareness of being in the middle of a space or mat, continuing the instruction on the slow, deep breaths, and feeling the sitting bones and straightening the spine.

If teaching the respect breath is too complex, have the children simply brush up the front of their trunk with their hands as they breathe in, and down as they breathe out. Model sitting up straight by first slumping over, then sitting up, and see if they can hold straight for a breath. Have them wiggle their bottoms to feel their sitting bones, if rocking is too much.

Warm-up. The essentials of the Boat for respect are teaching the coordination of movement and breath—not too fast or too slow—which can be a challenge for dysregulated children. Slow down the instruction by doing just a few back and forth "rows," or sit right next to a child and do the movements alongside them.

Poses. The essentials are your continued instruction of the mountain and that being steady is respectful to yourself and others. The poem with or without clapping is an excellent mnemonic.

Game. The essentials for the Stop game are establishing staying in your space and being in control. If you are very concerned about safety, honor that by simply playing the game with walking and stopping on the mat or confined space. Repeat this until safety is mastered, then consider more freedom of movement.

Rest. The essentials for respectful rest time are utilizing the rain and the puddle as a transition, learning to lay still with awareness of the body on the mat/space, and introduction of a story. For some, just resting in puddle might be enough, pointing out that respect for the body is happening. For restless children, keep the rest time short and point out even a few seconds of stillness with praise. Another option is to sit next to a child and say, "I am going to breathe here and help you be still." The story can simply be picturing the blue sky and warm sun shining on you.

Centering/Close. The essentials for closing are creating steadiness and respect for the transition, including restoring the room. You can have your group or child do as much or as little as is reasonable. If he/she/they can sit, then stand and leave the space as a steady mountain, that is a success.

Teaching and Using Respect at Home

Recommended Essentials for Respect at Home

Mountain, puddle, chime
Explicit teaching by word and example
Insisting through limit setting

Thus far, the book has introduced you to the foundational poses mountain and puddle, and the use of a chime to encourage deep breathing and attentiveness in your home. These can continue to support the teachings on respect. Many disrespectful mistakes happen when family members are physically or emotionally unsteady due to the small and big problems of life. The chime sound can "bring you back" to a calmer center, and even one deep breath can allow a pause that then can make respect easier. Becoming a mountain, or utilizing the puddle pose with a breath, can physically quiet a body and mind that may be heightened. Many adults truly appreciate the practices for themselves. Try incorporating them into a routine time, such as before dinner or bedtime.

As a parent, you are the most powerful teacher of respect your child will ever have: Your child learns from your words, your tone of voice, your body language, your choices. Establishing the intention to be "caring, gentle, and serious" in your treatment of your child is a conscious and worthy endeavor, challenging as it may be. If you can have this as a steady beacon, those thousands of hours of instruction in respect will happen through you and in your home. I continue to hold this intention as a mother and grandmother, and have been surprised at how often I have felt called to model, and insist on, respect in my family relationships. It is something that has to be continually practiced with self-awareness and control.

This teaching of respect happens by showing care and gentleness to yourself, other family members, and all the things of this world by never intentionally harming, sincerely apologizing when harm occurs, and practicing basic kindness. Seriousness is taught by treating the concept of respect itself with the highest regard and insisting on its practice—sometimes necessarily through limit setting.

In my inquiry on respect, I see that the most common confusion for children is being with adults who do not practice respect and do not limit set when a child is disrespectful. A lack of practice can be evidenced by sarcasm, unkind jokes, put downs, and hurtful discipline. Lack of limit setting is failing to say something or act when disrespect is witnessed. Won't you join me in taking a stand in support of respect, by being careful to avoid such confusion and saying, "That is not respectful. I always treat you with respect and expect you to treat me with respect;" or requiring a "time in with a breath" or a "time out with a breath" for times when respect is not practiced?

Chapter THREE
Calm

The Calm Song

I am calm
I am calm
Quiet
Steady
No matter what happens
I can become
Quiet
Steady

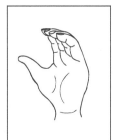

What can calm—as a word, a concept, and a skill—offer children today? It is easy to overlook, take for granted, or dismiss as too basic; and yet a child who is unquiet, unsteady, or unable to be soothed, can have great difficulty being safe and settling themselves enough to learn, manage emotions, and solve problems. Consequently, the ability to maintain calm in the body, mind, and heart with the help of the breath is a powerful practice and a key to resiliency for all children. A child who practices calm is more available to themselves, others, and the everyday challenges of growing up.

My inquiry about, and interest in, teaching calm grew from concern for the increasing number of children I was meeting whose bodies were regularly unsteady, whose minds were noticeably distracted, and whose hearts were reactive to emotion, with few coping skills for such challenges. Although all children are enjoyably rambunctious at times, from a skill development perspective, quiet steadiness in appropriate settings can be learned and, I would argue, should be taught to all children from an early age. This allows children to fully engage and navigate themselves and their relationships more smoothly and successfully, even when people and circumstances around them are chaotic. Skillfully calm children grow into skillfully calm adults who practice civility and clear thinking.

Developing such skillfulness in calm begins with developing self-awareness regarding the body, the mind, and the heart. The calm breath(s) taught throughout *Calm and Alert*—which encourage attentiveness to a slow, deep inhale, and a slow, deep exhale—are the beginning and foundation. Even one conscious calm breath allows a person of any age a chance to pause, notice their body, mind, and heart, and allows the nervous system a nanosecond of rest and reset. It offers a young person time to ask, "How am I right now?" and make adjustments if needed. Most children and adults I have served welcome the opportunity to reclaim a moment of innate calm, and find it satisfying.

With the calm breath practice established, the learning about calm can continue in the body. With the help of the movements and poses such as mountain and puddle, even children with special needs can come to notice when their body is quiet and steady, and utilize skill in becoming calm when they notice they are not. This allows any child the hope that they *can* control their bodies, and regain control if they have become unsteady. It is an antidote to organic or habitual dysregulation and ensuing discouragement I have seen in too many children who come to believe they can never be in control. Being able to take a calm breath and practice mindful effort in the body, even imperfectly for a few moments, creates what I call "the great feeling of being safe and in control."

A calm body then allows skillfulness in having a calm mind possible. Although the opportunities offered children on screens can be enriching, the riveting, competitive, and sometimes violent imagery can agitate the susceptible young mind, sometimes habitually. This kind of preoccupied, agitated mind then has trouble focusing on things in real time and can create unease for children. The calm skills offered here allow a child to use the breath to find a quieter, steadier place in the mind, and turn away from other distractions. The skillful calm mind notices thoughts and images, and then can choose to turn the attention to those appropriate "thoughtscapes" that are healthier.

A calm body and mind can then help the heart manage emotions better. Although the human heart cannot avoid troubles and ensuing emotion, the pitfalls of emotional dysregulation (e.g., reactivity, aggression, inability to self-soothe) can be prevented with instruction. The skills grow from the teaching of the six basic emotions (happy, sad, scared, angry, surprised, disgusted), the reality that they can range in intensity depending on circumstance, and the skill that "no matter what happens, I can become calm." A skillfully calm child knows that any problem can be faced without letting emotion go to an extreme. This instruction has had a validating impact on the children who are already skillfully calm, and has given dysregulated children tools to practice becoming calm.

Calm, self-soothing skills are offered each class during rest time. These include being aware of troubling thoughts and feelings, imagining placing them aside for a time, picturing a comforting place of beauty, finding a "quiet, steady place" inside them, and abiding there for a time. It is a time to also teach "this is what calm feels like," both for those who may already know and especially for children who lack rudimentary skills in calming and soothing. Ultimately, the real beauty of the teaching is that each child's inner calm becomes a resource they can reliably trust when the winds of life blow.

Calm Concepts

Calm = quiet and steady
Quiet = still and silent
Steady = grounded and in control

I can be calm or become calm
no matter what happens.

Teaching Calm as a Class

Begin
Centering
Warm-up
Poses
Game
Rest
Centering/Close

Lesson 3: Calm

Begin. With children sitting at tables or on the floor, remind them of past teaching in the *Calm and Alert* class: Our bodies, minds, and breath help us; we are respectful to ourselves, others, and all things; and we start class with the chime practice. Cue them to sit up straight, then:

Chime Practice

Ring chime, listen as long as you can
Lead children in 3–5 slow, deep breaths
Ring chime, listen as long as you can

As the chime sound diminishes, have them put their hands over their hearts and ask: "Can you feel a calm inside? We are going to learn about being and becoming calm today, and our song will teach us what calm means." Then line by line, teach them the Calm song or recite it as a poem. If you want to incorporate simple hand movements (other than ASL, found in a dictionary): place palms down, open hands in air in front of chest as you sing the first two lines; place fingers to mouth for "quiet" and fingers to belly area for "steady;" shrug shoulders with hands outstretched for "no matter what happens;" repeat motions for quiet and steady at end.

Calm Song

I am calm
I am calm
Quiet
Steady
No matter what happens
I can become
Quiet
Steady

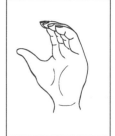

Have pictures of the six basic feelings and a paint chip with gradations of color from light to dark ready (I recommend pink to red). Ask the children what these pictures show (feelings) and have them name each one as you show them individually. Say, "Everyone has feelings about lots of different things and we can be calm no matter what feeling we have." Show them the paint chip, point to the palest color, and say, "This is the calm zone of feelings. Sometimes feelings can get into the strong zone," (bring your finger up to the darkest color) "but we will learn how to help our feelings stay in the calm zone" (bring finger back down to pink). Place your finger on the darkest color; take a calm breath in and as you exhale bring your finger to the palest color.

Remind the children about how respectfully we moved the furniture and got our mats from the mat bins last time, and review all the steps by modeling again yourself. Monitor the process carefully by pointing out all the children who are respectful and safe, to continue the instruction from the respect lesson. If one or more parts of the process are unskillful, take the time to re-teach. Other highlights can be noticing any child who remains calm while mats are being rolled out and problems are solved.

Centering. Once everyone is sitting in the middle of their rolled-out mats cross-legged, remind the children of their spines (use picture again) and have them take one outstretched thumb and feel their spine. Ask, "Is your spine straight? Let's check." Then have them touch the top of their heads and imagine there is a string pulling them up to straight. You can be sitting or standing. Also remind them of their sitting bones that keep them steady.

Include the Hoberman sphere by taking it in your hand and calling it your breathing ball, which will teach us how to breathe. (It is usually exciting.) Say, "Let's remember the calm breath. Put your hands on your belly and watch the sphere get as big as it can be as you breathe in, then become small as it can be as you breathe out." Take a few calm breaths this way with the help of the sphere. Then instruct them to put their hands on their hearts and ask, "Can you notice calm inside?" To further enhance instruction, have the children make a fist and hold it up in the air with a bent elbow as you model. Say, "This fist is a mini brain. When you take a calm breath you give your brain a hug." Take your other hand and place it at the inside of the bent elbow.

Take a calm breath in and slowly bring the hand up to gently cover and "hug" the mini brain. Have the children do it with you.

Calm breath: Sit up straight, take a deep breath in and out.

Warm-up. Remind the children about the Boat warm-up from last time, and that this time we will be noticing calm and becoming calm as we practice.

Boat

Sit up straight with legs out in front of you. Prepare for your boat trip by reaching your arms up overhead and grabbing a life jacket; then pretend to put it on, keeping you safe. Twist to one side and grab a cushion, then twist to the other side and grab a blanket to keep you warm and comfortable in your boat. Reach behind you and grab a healthy snack. Grab your pretend oars in the air in front of your chest. Breathe in and sit up straight and slightly back, breathe out and bring the oars forward. Then repeat, moving forward and back a few times with the breath until you reach your destination.

Once you have established a rhythm and the group is steady, ask them to say the word "quiet" as they bend forward and "steady" as they sit up, and repeat a few times. Slowly speed up the pace until it becomes fast (and possibly silly), then begin to slow it down again until you stop. When finished say, "We just practiced being not calm, then becoming calm—did you feel it?" Point out we also had a good time without losing control.

Poses. Now have the children step out of their boats and squat in the middle of their mats for the calm frog, then tree climber to bring the children to standing. If your group is stable, you can also add the tree before moving into the school tools.

Frog/Tree

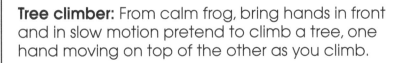

Calm frog: Squat with feet flat (or what is possible), knees wide, arms in between legs, hands touching floor. Be "so still that nothing can catch you on the edge of the pond" and take deep breaths.

Tree climber: From calm frog, bring hands in front and in slow motion pretend to climb a tree, one hand moving on top of the other as you climb.

Tree: Start in mountain. Tap on leg and put all weight on this leg. Point opposite toe and rest it next to standing leg on floor. Turn knee of pointed toe foot out to side. If steady here, try raising the bent knee leg up and rest foot on calf or thigh (not knee). If unsteady, bring foot down to floor. Repeat on other side.

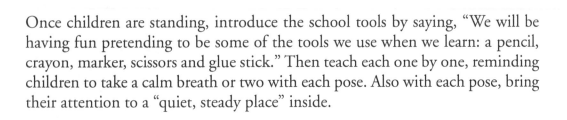

Once children are standing, introduce the school tools by saying, "We will be having fun pretending to be some of the tools we use when we learn: a pencil, crayon, marker, scissors and glue stick." Then teach each one by one, reminding children to take a calm breath or two with each pose. Also with each pose, bring their attention to a "quiet, steady place" inside.

Calm School Tools

Calm pencil: Start in standing mountain. Inhale, arms up overhead bringing hands together into a point like a pencil. Remain steady.

Calm crayon: Like pencil above except pointed hands rest on to top of head.

Calm marker: Start in standing mountain. Bring elbows close into sides, forearms folded to chest, thumbs touching shoulders. Remain steady; imagine being a marker with the cap on.

Calm scissors: Start in standing mountain. Inhale, raise arms overhead and cross hands so backs of hands are touching. Remain steady; imagine being scissors resting.

Calm glue stick: Start in standing mountain. Raise arms up overhead, flat palms facing ceiling—a glue stick with cap on. Remain steady, calm breaths.

Game. Remind the children of the Stop game we played last time, and how we practiced respect for ourselves and others by staying in our space and being safe. Say, "Every game we play, we have the great feeling of being safe and in control. It makes games fun. Today we will be practicing playing a game which takes us off our mats." To encourage mastery, I always practice the movements required by the game on the mat before getting off the mats, so for Mountain/Cloud, practice walking like a cloud on the mat and then standing like a mountain. Then model how that will look as we step off our mats: Point out how steady your body is as you walk; tell them you can feel your calm inside as you move.

Mountain/Cloud

Have child/children stand like a mountain in the middle of the mat or space. After teaching "mountain" and "cloud" (standing, hugging arms around yourself, and walking slowly and respectfully like a floating cloud) tell children we will now play the mountain/cloud game.

Whenever you say "mountain" the children are to stand like a mountain wherever they are. Whenever you say "cloud" they are to float around the room.

You can leave many seconds or just a few between words. You can add other poses as children become adept.

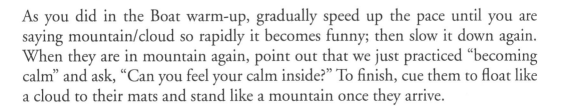

As you did in the Boat warm-up, gradually speed up the pace until you are saying mountain/cloud so rapidly it becomes funny; then slow it down again. When they are in mountain again, point out that we just practiced "becoming calm" and ask, "Can you feel your calm inside?" To finish, cue them to float like a cloud to their mats and stand like a mountain once they arrive.

Rest. Rest time then begins as the children take a breath in, bring hands overhead, wiggle their fingers to find their rain, and gently sprinkle themselves with their wiggly fingers as they come into a puddle. Continue your instruction about the puddle by saying, "Every part of you becomes calm in the puddle: your heart, your lungs, your spine, your mind." Then turn the lights down and put on quiet music if you wish. Have them lay on their backs for a rest-time visit to the garden.

Rest Time Script: The Garden

"Lay on your back and become still on your mat by using your deep, calm breaths. Notice your feet, legs, torso, arms, hands, neck, and head and become still. This is how we rest our bodies. Can you feel quiet and steady?

Now we will rest our minds and heart with a story:

Picture a beautiful blue sky and the sun shining down on you. Imagine a big field and see yourself walk, skip, run, or hop through the field. You hear, then see, a steady stream and walk beside it. The bubbling sounds seem to say 'lay all your cares in my waters' and you take any cares you have and imagine them washed away by the stream. You keep walking until you reach the gate of a beautiful garden.

See yourself push open the gate and step inside. Look around the garden: notice birds and butterflies, flowers and trees; feel the warm breeze on your cheek. Let the beauty and sounds remind you of a quiet, steady place you have inside you. Notice a table with healthy foods like fruits and vegetables, and clear water; and imagine eating and drinking with someone who cares about you."

Pause here and allow silence for a few minutes.

"Now we must say goodbye to your beautiful place, but we never have to leave our quiet, steady place—it is always with you. Walk back through the field to _____ (their present setting). Turn on your side and pause there. Bring your knees into your chest, wrap your arms around your knees and give yourself a hug and whisper: 'I am calm.' Now push yourself up to sitting."

Centering/Close. Once everyone is sitting cross-legged in the middle of their mats, have them put their hands on their bellies and take three calm breaths with your Hoberman sphere again as a visual. "Breathe in until my ball is as big as it can be; breathe out until it is as small as it can be." The sphere has enhanced instruction of the breath exponentially!

Remind the children of our practice of respecting our mats by coming to the back of our mats and rolling them up tightly before sitting like a little mountain with the mat between our legs. Continue your practice of checking with children before they stand to take their mats to the bin, this time asking, "Are you calm?" Supervise the process, reinforcing calm and respect as you see it, until furniture is moved and seats are resumed. End by singing the Calm song or reciting it as a poem. Then say, "I respect you," and expect the children to say the same to you.

Calm and Alert Lesson: Calm

Lesson 3

Grade/Group_____   Date_____

Materials needed:
Mats
Chime
Pictures of six feelings
Hoberman sphere
Paint chip

<u>Lesson</u>

Begin:
Chime
Calm song
Feeling instruction

Centering:
The calm breath with sphere (called breathing ball)
Use forearm/fist to illustrate calm breath's effect on brain

Warm-up:
Boat (all elements)

Poses:
Calm frog
Calm school tools: pencil, crayon, marker, glue stick, scissors

Game:
Mountain/Cloud: first time off mats

Rest:
Garden

Centering/Close:
Calm breath
Calm song

Teaching and Using Calm in Other Settings

Remember to read, if possible, the entire lesson offered previously to get a sense of all the calm foundations. Offered here are the recommended essentials and modifications, including a reminder that you can shorten, combine, or break up all class elements, but use the previous template as your guide.

Recommended Essentials for Calm

You can become calm: instilling hope and confidence
Be a calm role model: quiet, steady
The calm breath(s)
The puddle as a foundational pose
Explicitly teaching how calm feels

For many children with special needs such as ASD, behavioral challenges, trauma backgrounds, ADHD, or dysregulated adult role models, being and becoming calm is difficult and a very new experience. ("I can't feel it!" they tell me, and I believe them.) Some may believe it is not possible for them to be calm, become calm, nor have a sense of what calm feels like inside. My practice as a teacher has been to teach the skills with hope and confidence: Expect that any child, even with organic challenges, can learn to recognize the feeling of calm and practice some strategies for becoming calm when upset, even for short periods imperfectly. You are the calm role model; over time your messaging, "You can become calm," will have an effect.

Practicing the calm breath(s) and mastering the puddle are essentials for learning calm. The breath quiets the nervous system and the puddle pose gives each part of the body a quiet, steady experience. Both can be used as tools for adults who can request a dysregulated child to take a calm breath or go into the pose. Ideally a child can learn to independently take a calm breath or request the puddle when needed. Together, these offer a "time in" experience of visceral calming for the entire system in a way "time out" spaces or motor breaks cannot always offer a dysregulated child.

Once a child can practice these essentials, a teacher can explicitly explain: "This is calm;" or "This is what calm feels like;" or ask, "Can you feel a quiet, steady place inside?" "Where do you feel your calm?" As a role model yourself, you can also offer your calm while you wait for mastery: "I will sit next to you and lend you my calm," "Give me your hand and see if you can feel my calm," "I will wait with you until you become calm"—all can instill hope.

Modifying Class Elements

Begin. Reread and follow the recommendations from the Respect chapter about your space, and continue to spend the time needed to establish a calm routine as you get the room ready for practice. The essentials for "begin" as you teach calm are the chime practice, the song, and the instruction about feelings.

As you offer the chime practice consider ringing the chime ever so slightly and possibly only once at the start if the sound creates irritation for a child. Expect at least one calm breath. Ask: "Can you feel calm?" after the practice. Keep persisting until the practice is established as a routine.

The songs have been very effective for special populations—the Calm song in particular—and establish a mnemonic for skill mastery. Consider teaching just a few lines at a time. The line "no matter what happens" can create a segue to the instruction about feelings. The instruction concerning the six feelings and remaining in the "calm zone" can be done over multiple sessions. Start by simply exposing the children to the feeling pictures, then move to naming the feelings and what can cause feelings to arise, then teach the strength of feelings with the paint chip. Be sure to emphasize the point that every problem can be solved and "there is no need to let feelings get into the strong zone."

Centering. The essentials for centering in the teaching of calm are the calm breath(s), utilizing the Hoberman sphere to be sure the children are breathing deeply, and offering the mini brain illustration with your arm/fist to teach the effects of the breath. For some children, the calm breath is uninteresting, unmotivating, or difficult to use. The Hoberman sphere can make it more entertaining, the mini brain gives them more movement, and you may want to experiment with some of the other calm breaths now (which will be introduced in greater detail in later chapters).

Calm Breaths (5)

1. **Calm breath:** Sit up straight, place hands on belly, take a deep, slow breath in and out.

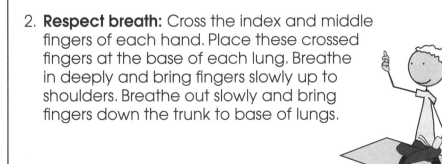

2. **Respect breath:** Cross the index and middle fingers of each hand. Place these crossed fingers at the base of each lung. Breathe in deeply and bring fingers slowly up to shoulders. Breathe out slowly and bring fingers down the trunk to base of lungs.

3. **Book breath:** Sit up straight and place index finger in the air. Breathe in to the count of three while moving finger horizontally to right. Breathe out to count of three, moving finger down toward floor. Breathe in to count of three, moving finger horizontally to left. Breathe out to count of three, moving finger up toward ceiling. This can also be done as an alert breath by making the same square shape with quick breaths in and out.

4. **M and M breath:** Sit up straight and place hand on chest. Take a deep breath in, close mouth, and make the "m" sound quietly as you exhale. Repeat; then ask: "Can you feel the sound making you calm?"

hummm

5. **Heart breath:** Sit up straight and place hands on top of head with curved fingers. Take a deep breath in and bring hands up in a curving motion like the top of a heart shape; breathe out and arch hands as they come down into the point of the heart. This can also be done as an alert breath with same movements but quick breaths in and out.

Also consider letting the child make up their own calm breaths—the slow, deep inhalation and exhalation is the essential skill, the imagery less important except as a motivator.

Warm-up. The essentials of the Boat warm-up for calm instruction are the slow, steady movement, the repetition of the words "quiet, steady" to teach the definition and increase vocabulary, and the beginning instruction on "becoming calm" after excitement as you speed up and slow down the rowing. Take one at a time if needed for your population.

Poses. The essentials for poses in the instruction of calm is offering a few poses that require a quiet steadfastness, which allows you to point out when children are calm or ask if they feel calm. For a highly-active child, consider starting with the puddle to establish calm, then move to the mountain before teaching new poses such as the frog or the school tools.

Game. The essentials for the game in teaching calm are emphasizing being quiet and steady "no matter what happens." The mountain/cloud game can be played on the mats but with all the other elements of starting/stopping, being in control, becoming excited, then becoming calm. Be sure to end the game by standing like a mountain, then rain, then puddle.

Rest. For dysregulated children, learning to become still for a short time and recognizing their "quiet, steady place" are the essentials and can take many months, even years, for mastery. Your calm creates the foundational energy for the teaching, as the young person sees your steadiness, hears your quiet voice, and senses your confidence that calm can be found. With a smaller group or individually, you can sit near the child (adjust if appropriate) and give specific feedback. Here are some ideas:

Rest Time Feedback Ideas

- **Sit near the child and say:** "I see your _____ (name one body part) is/are still."

- **Say:** "Let's take a calm breath together and see if we can become calmer."

- **Ask:** "Is your body on your mat?" or "Can you feel that you are not still?"

- **Ask:** "Where do you feel calm right now?" or "Can you say 'quiet, steady' with me?"

After a time, move on to encouraging the child to picture something beautiful, even if they cannot be still. You can use the entire script as offered, or just highlight the sky, the field, the quiet, steady stream, and the garden. Say, "The beautiful _____ is teaching us to notice the quiet, steady place we have inside."

Centering/Close. The essentials of centering for calm at the end of the session are reorienting the child to the transition out of practice and holding onto any calm awareness that may have been learned. Follow the routines already established, take calm breaths with the breathing ball, and sing or recite the Calm song at the end. With special populations, the transition out of practice can become unsteady, so bringing awareness to the calm inside as things change can be a "teachable moment."

Teaching and Using Calm at Home

Recommended Essentials
for Calm at Home

You can expect your child to be calm
You can teach a child to become calm when emotional
The power of calm in parenting
Offering a calm resting place in your home

The recommended essentials from the previous chapter—the calm breath, the use of the chime, and the mountain and puddle poses—continue to be supportive essentials for the practice of calm in your home. I am hoping this chapter and this section will support you in your efforts to provide a calm home for your family at a time when this may feel culturally unsupported. A calm home teaches children that the world is a safe place, that problems can be faced with courage, and that they can rely on a strong center within them to overcome difficulty.

The first two essentials—that you can expect your child to be calm and become calm—are the foundation of physical and emotional regulation, which is a well-documented key to every success in life. From a young age, children can learn the value of calm by your praise when they are so, your limit setting when they are not so, and (when appropriate) your disapproval when they show extreme emotion or out-of-control behavior. Over time, they can learn to notice that "quiet, steady place" and feel proud of being regulated, even if other people or events around them may be dysregulated.

Although it is a great responsibility, the power of your calm as a parent cannot be underestimated. Your child is watching you constantly and learning "this is how people behave." If you handle problems steadily, have emotions without losing control, discipline without harm, and practice patience, you will be your child's best teacher. Even if you cannot guarantee the calm of other family members, your own commitment to your practice of calm will help establish the resting place highlighted in the last essential. A calm resting place in the home is one in which children sense love and safety and are not emotionally taxed by fear, uncertainty, or overstimulation. One calm adult—you—can offer such a sanctuary. Take a calm breath and know you are on your way.

Chapter FOUR

Alert

Alert Song

I am alert
I am alert
Awake
Ready to learn
Every day at home
Every day at school
Awake
Ready to learn

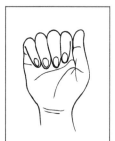

Anyone who has ever had the pleasure of spending time with an alert child, one who is rested, awake, and ready for any task, knows the value of this state of being. Being alert has many advantages: It makes learning easier, helps us approach tasks with optimism, encourages mindful effort in movement, increases the ability to hold and maintain attention and focus, and develops the ability to change a mind state toward the positive. Coupled with calmness, alertness allows any child to take in and take on the enjoyment and challenges of living each day.

Its opposite—lethargy, fatigue, and negative mind states—make learning, trying new things, problem solving, and physical and other activity difficult. For children who are sleep deprived, who spend more than the recommended two hours or less in front of a screen and its ensuing inactivity (Rogers & Motyka,

2009), who are not encouraged to be actively engaged in healthy activities at home or who are chronically taxed by stress, a non-alert state can become habitual. Hence the explicit teaching regarding alertness is the assertion that you can be and become more alert through conscious use of the body, mind, and breath. This has the potential to give even habitually tired children the hope that they can feel better, even for a short time, by practice.

Developmentally, all children struggle (some more than others) with learning to manage barriers to alertness and the consequential reluctance to do what is expected. These barriers include minor somatic complaints (congestion, tummy aches, headache), fatigue (short term or chronic), negative thoughts about a task ("I don't want to!"), and distractibility (both internal and external). The alert skills are developed starting with the benefits of erect posture for the body and brain, and the awareness that just sitting up straight can help a person feel more awake. The alert breaths are energizing and viscerally teach children that a quick inhale/exhale can nourish a tired body and brain in a moment. These foundations then allow the instruction about how positive thoughts (clear) encourage alertness, while negative thoughts (muddy) encourage discouragement and reluctance.

The fruit of the teaching for well-rested and naturally alert children is the validation that this state is fun, happy, and makes tasks more enjoyable. For children who struggle to be alert, the skills offer them the chance to change the way they feel by practicing and the hope that they can be empowered to feel better by sitting up straight, taking a breath, and having a clear thought.

Alert Concepts

Awake = eyes open, sitting straight
Ready = prepared and willing

I can be alert or become alert when needed.

Teaching Alert as a Class

Begin
Centering
Warm-up
Poses
Game
Rest
Centering/Close

Lesson 4: Alert

Begin. If this is indeed your fourth lesson, you should be able to draw from past instruction about respect and calm, and start to see the establishment of class routines. Remind the children of all we have learned thus far and that today we will be learning more about alert: what it is, how it feels, and how we can be more alert.

As they sit steady and ready, hold your chime and remind them of all we have learned from the chime so far about listening to the sound and being calm. Tell them that the chime can also teach us about how to be more awake and ready. Say, "Put your eyes on me. Your eyes send messages to your brain about what is important. Your eyes right now are telling your brain that the chime and listening are important." As you ring the chime say, "Are you awake right now as you listen? How long can you listen?" As you lead them in the breaths, remind them that the air we bring into our bodies also helps us be ready for anything we have to do. With the final chime sound, notice children who appear awake and attentive. Ask, "How do you feel right now?" as you close.

Chime Practice

Ring chime, listen as long as you can
Lead children in 3–5 slow, deep breaths
Ring chime, listen as long as you can

Teach the Alert song/poem line by line. It would be beneficial to do the alert movement you will later use for the breath as you sing the word "alert," because it inherently offers a physical reminder of the alert concept.

Alert Sign

Place index and middle fingers on thumbs of each hand. Place these fingers alongside of eyes on each side. Open the fingers wide as you say/sing "alert."

Alert Song

I am alert
I am alert
Awake
Ready to learn
Every day at home
Every day at school
Awake
Ready to learn

After the song, say, "It is funny to say that we need to be awake, isn't it, because no one right now is asleep! But we can feel tired and grumpy, and then we might not want to do things. To get the feeling of alertness, and how easy it is to help ourselves, we are going to play a quick game called 'On and Off.'"

On and Off

Hold up your on/off switch. Illustrate that it can
be clicked to "on" or "off." Say, "When our inside
switch is off, we feel grumpy and tired and it
makes us unready. When our inside switch is on,
we feel happy and ready. We are going to notice what on and
off feel like right now. When I click the switch off, pretend you
are tired and grumpy by putting your head down and slumping
over. When I click the switch on, take a quick breath in and sit
up straight."

Then click the switch on and off a few times, getting faster
each round. The last time, keep it on "on" and say the word "on"
multiple times. Ask, "Can you feel what alert feels like? This is
'on,' and when we have jobs to do we need to have our inside
switch on."

Continue your teaching by saying, "Now let's stay alert as we get the room ready
for our practice. An alert person watches everything they do: their body, the
space and things around them, other people." Then lead the group in moving
the furniture, getting their mats, and rolling them out in rows as practiced in
earlier lessons.

Centering. Once the children are sitting cross-legged in the center of their mats,
remind them of past learning (or teach it again—see previous lessons): sitting
bones keeping them steady, straight spine. Emphasize that a straight spine is the
first thing to do to become alert. Remind them to put their hands on the top of
their heads and reach up as if a string was pulling them, and you may also add a
rolling of the shoulders up, back and down as a straightener. Ask them to smile
and feel the goodness of a straight spine.

As you teach the first alert breath, have the Hoberman sphere ready. Illustrate
again how calm breaths come in and out slowly by expanding and collapsing the
sphere slowly. Then illustrate the quick in and out breath by modeling it and
opening and closing the sphere quickly. I never encourage children to take more
than a few alert breaths at a time, and teach that they should stop immediately

if they feel dizzy. Have them put their hand on their heart and notice an alert feeling inside.

Alert breath: Place index and middle fingers on thumbs of each hand. Place these fingers alongside of eyes on each side. Take a quick breath in, open the eyes wide, and splay fingers away from thumb while bringing hands up toward ceiling. Bring hands back down with exhale.

To enhance instruction, use again your fist in the air with a bent elbow as a mini brain, and ask the children to do the same. Remind them that we learned last time that calm breaths are a hug to the brain (other hand starts at the elbow bend, slowly comes up the forearm then hugs the mini brain and comes down). Illustrate the effect of alert breaths by starting with hand back at the elbow crease, and as you take in an alert breath shoot hand up to mini brain and quickly down again. Alert breaths wake up our brains, making us ready for anything!

Warm-up. Introduce the warm-up Blast Off as a way to wake up the whole body for the rest of our practice together. Note that in this warm-up our bodies will be moving and changing, but we will keep our steadiness.

Blast Off

Sit on your mat with your feet flat in front of you, knees bent. Place your hands behind your trunk: feel steady here. Breathe out and slowly bring your knees down to the right. Breathe in, bring your knees back up. Breathe out and bring them over to the left. Go back and forth two times. This movement will be the countdown for the blast off—starting with 10 and knees to right, nine with knees to left, back and forth slowly until zero.

For blast off: Knees stay to the right as you push up onto your knees with your right hand near your right hip for support, your left hand swinging up and over to the right. Then slowly come down and swing knees to left for blast off on the left side. Come up onto your left knees, your left hand near your hip for support, your right arm swinging up and over to the left.

Pause the group for a moment afterwards, with bottoms on their mats, and ask them how they feel. Praise children's steadiness while moving throughout the movement.

Poses. Start the pose sequences in this lesson with the calm frog (as learned in the last lesson) as a foundation of steadiness in the transition from sitting to standing. Then teach the alert frog by bringing their attention to their feet on the mat, hopping but remaining steady with an alert breath in, and challenging them to land back on the spot they started. Do three alert frogs and praise those who do not fall over or become silly for being steady. On the fourth alert frog have them hop up to standing. Once the calm, then alert frog is mastered, it can be the way you always bring the children to standing.

Frog: Squat with feet flat (or what is possible), knees wide, arms in between legs, hands touching floor.

Calm frog: Be as steady as possible, not moving, deep breaths.

Alert frog: Hop up with a quick breath in, down with a quick breath out.

Building on the calm school tools from the last lesson, start each of the school tools with the calm version to create a steady pause, then offer three alert versions of each, if time allows.

School Tools

Calm pencil: Start in standing mountain. Inhale, arms up overhead bringing hands together into a point like a pencil. Remain steady.

Alert pencil: Breathe in, stay straight; exhale, bend to right; inhale, center; exhale, bend left—a pencil writing.

Calm crayon: Like pencil above except pointed hands rest on top of head.

Alert crayon: Like alert pencil—moving side to side with breath; imagine coloring.

Calm marker: Start in standing mountain. Bring elbows close into sides, forearms folded to chest, thumbs touching shoulders. Remain steady; imagine being a marker with the cap on.

Alert marker: With an alert breath in, pop cap off by bringing arms quickly to ceiling; exhale, pop cap back on by bringing them down to calm position.

Calm scissors: Start in standing mountain. Inhale, raise arms overhead and cross hands so backs of hands are touching. Remain steady; imagine being scissors resting.

Alert scissors: Alert breath in, arms come out wide in a "V" shape; exhale, bring arms back to center and clap hands—a scissors cutting.

Calm glue stick: Start in standing mountain. Raise arms up overhead, flat palms facing ceiling—a glue stick with the cap on. Remain steady, calm breaths.

Alert glue stick: Keeping steady with feet unmoving, breathe in and rotate just the trunk to the right in a circle, imagining gluing the ceiling; exhale while finishing circle. Go the other way with next breath, staying as straight as possible.

Celebrate the work of the alert movements. As you notice signs of fatigue, point out that sometimes tasks are hard, tiring, or we might not want to do them, but being alert can make it easier.

Game. The game in this lesson helps children practice being alert while moving and having fun, by being respectfully awake to ourselves and the space we move in, and ready to interact and touch others as we play. If you would like to begin using music for cueing, introduce the practice of using lively, alert music for movement, and stopping when the music stops, which requires attentive listening. Establish again the expectation that every part of the game is safe and in control, and limit set if necessary. To add more instruction about safe, respectful touching before you begin the game, encourage anyone who does not want to be touched to say "please don't touch me" during the game.

Touch One

Have child/children stand like a mountain in the middle of the mat or space. Put on lively music and give an instruction to move: hopping, skipping, or galloping (pick one). When the music stops, children freeze.

You then say: "Touch one_____
(name a safe body part—pinky finger, toe, etc.)
to someone else's _____ (same safe body part)." Say, "If you feel respected, smile at the person you are touching." In a school setting, it is best to use "elbow" and "shoulder" to help instruct that these are the safest, most respectful ways to touch someone. Emphasize respectful touching and being in control.

End the game by having the children come back to their mats and stand like a mountain.

Rest. Rest time again begins as the children take a breath in, bring hands overhead, wiggle their fingers to find their rain, and gently sprinkle themselves with their wiggly fingers as they come into a puddle. Your instruction about the puddle today, now that it is a (hopefully) established pose, is that after all the excitement of movement and feeling alert, it is now time to become calm and rest. Both are important. Then turn the lights down, put on quiet music if you wish, and have them lay on their backs for rest time.

The selection of the ocean for this lesson is purposeful because the ocean is always alert and the perfect teacher for alert: moving, flowing, waves rising, cresting then crashing.

Rest Time Script: The Ocean

"Lay on your back and become still on your mat by using your deep, calm breaths. Notice your feet, legs, torso, arms, hands, neck, and head, and lay without moving. This is how we rest our bodies.

Now we will rest our minds and heart with a story:

"Picture a beautiful blue sky and the sun shining down on you. Imagine a big field and see yourself walk, skip, run, or hop through the field. You hear, then see, a steady stream and walk beside it. The bubbling sounds seem to say 'lay all your cares in my waters' and you take any cares you have and imagine them washed away by the stream. Today we will be visiting the ocean.

See yourself step onto a sandy beach, and feel the warm sand on your feet. Imagine yourself walking or running to the edge of the water. Notice how alert the ocean is as it moves and the waves rise, crest, and crash over and over. Notice the air, the sun, the smells. Let the beauty and sounds remind you of a quiet, steady place you have inside you."

Pause here and allow silence for a few minutes.

"Now it is time to say goodbye to your beautiful place, but we never have to leave our quiet, steady place—it is always with you. Say goodbye to the ocean and imagine walking back over the sand to the field. Thank the quiet, steady stream for holding your troubles. Head back to _____ (their present setting). Turn on your side and pause there. Bring your knees into your chest, wrap your arms around your knees and give yourself a hug. Now push yourself up to sitting."

Centering/Close. Cue the children to sit back up and to notice how they feel. Teach them that sometimes we may feel tired after rest time, especially if we do not feel well or did not sleep well last night, but we can alert our bodies and mind with our breath. Lead the group in three alert breaths, utilizing the Hoberman sphere as a support.

You should begin to see the fruits of earlier instruction here, as children more smoothly sit up, practice the breaths, come to the back of their mats, roll their mats, and return the room to its original orientation. When the group is ready, rather than calling individual children who are sitting "like a little mountain with the mat between their legs, steady," begin to ask the children to assess whether they are "steady and ready." Allow them to answer the question themselves and return their mats.

If the group still needs a high level of supervision, consider using the chime as a motivator.

Using the Chime to Further the Establishment of Stable Routines

- "I am going to ring the chime three times. See if you can be sitting up on your mat by the last chime sound."

- "I am going to ring the chime five times. See if everyone can be back in their seats by the final chime sound."

- "I am going to keep ringing my chime until everyone is _____ (quiet, steady, lining up, back at their seats, safe, etc.)."

End the lesson by singing/reciting the Alert song, and say, "I respect you" to the class.

Calm and Alert Lesson: Alert

Lesson 4

Grade/Group_____   Date_____

Materials needed:
On/Off Switch

Lesson

Begin:
Alert song

Centering:
The alert breath
Use arm/hand to illustrate effect of alert breaths on brain

Warm-up:
Blast Off

Poses:
Alert frog
Calm and alert school tools

Game:
Touch One

Rest:
Ocean

Centering/Close:
Alert breath
Alert song

Teaching and Using Alert in Other Settings

You are familiar now with the understanding that reading the aforementioned class section will establish your understanding of how the chapter topic, in this case, "alert," is approached and taught generally to any group of children. This section will help you focus on the essentials and help you modify the instruction for your population in whatever setting you find yourself and the children you serve in.

Recommended Essentials for Alert

Energy management: calm and alert
The difference between alert and hyperactive
Feeling alert: letting your body, mind, and breath help you
Thoughts as a help or hindrance
Finding needed rest

For many children with any kind of special needs, learning what alert is and how it feels is a unique challenge because their emotional and physical regulation can swing to extremes of lethargy or hyperactivity and become their habitual baseline. For children who tend toward hyperactivity (e.g., the ones who say "I am always hyper"), the instruction is new, difficult at first, and critical.

The first essential assumes the basic concepts of alert have been taught and a child has been asked to notice what alert might feel like for them. Then you can begin the valuable teaching that it feels good and helps us when we are both calm *and* alert—they are not mutually exclusive. This allows a child to understand the difference between an inner engine that is in high gear and one that is on the proper gear for optimal functioning. High gear: moving constantly, making noises, talking incessantly, distractible, out of control (hyperactive). Proper gear: eyes are open, body in control, attending, willing to take on a task (alert). The hope is that the development of self-awareness (are you calm? are you alert?) will lead to the ability to cope with or change an inner state, the basis for what is called energy management.

The empowering message for children is that you can use your body (sitting up straight), mind (clear thoughts), and breath (calm or alert breaths) to help yourself feel better and do better. There will be further instruction in the next chapter on the skillful use of thoughts, but I want to highlight here the instruction that you can change muddy thoughts that get in the way of being alert.

Thoughts that hinder or help with alert:

Hinder	**Help**
I am always hyper	I am calm and alert
I am too tired	I can become alert
I don't want to	I will try
I can't do this	I can do this

The final essential is the importance of understanding rest, which will be explored in more depth in the following section for parents. If a child is physically exhausted, sleep deprived, or chronically taxed emotionally, it will be very difficult for them to become rested and fully alert with just a straight spine or a few breaths. To state the obvious, they should be offered the rest they need if possible. If not possible, the rest time offered here is a start, and the instruction a ray of hope for feeling a bit better.

Modifying Class Elements

Begin. Continue to build on all the particular routines you may have established for your setting, remembering you are hoping to teach the children a rhythm for the start of practice. If the chime has worked well, use it now to plant the seed of learning that the sound can wake us up and keep us awake as we listen, while the calm breaths help us become steady as we start. Take any liberty appropriate with the words to the song/poem to match your setting. For example, replace "ready to learn" with "ready to work/play" and "every day at school" with "every day in _____(speech, OT, sports)." The On and Off switch game might be too stimulating—if you do not want to give up on it, simply show your children the switch with the promise that "if everyone is calm enough, we can try it next time." Try doing the on/off one time and build on it in the days ahead.

Centering. Always be sure everyone is as settled and steady as possible here, utilizing the straight spine, the sitting bones instruction, and the calm breaths as the baseline. If your population easily becomes aroused, try introducing just one alert breath to begin the instruction. If a child wants to repeatedly breathe rapidly, limit set with the teaching that this is not a healthy practice for them, and why.

Warm-up. Blast Off requires some self-control or the instruction can be confusing. Start with the back and forth movements being slow and steady, and do not move forward until this is so. If you are concerned about even introducing Blast Off, trust yourself and offer the Boat again and again until self-control is better established. You can still weave in the instruction about alert by making the back and forth movements increasingly faster paced, and see if the children feel an alert steadiness.

Poses. If you are modifying the number of poses offered, choose one or two that would be enjoyable. For a highly dysregulated child, stick with pencil, crayon, or marker. If you have the time to individually work with a child who is unsteady and hyperactive, repeated practice of the frogs with explicit feedback after each alert frog can be very effective. And remember, the mountain pose is an untiring comfort to return to whenever needed.

Game. If safety is an issue and social skills are seriously lagging, return to the Mountain/Cloud game rather than Touch One. If you want to begin instruction on safe and alert touching of others using the Mountain/Cloud game, when they do the cloud, have the children just lightly touch on the shoulders, and keep the pace of the game slow. (There will be more social skill instruction in the Social Time chapter.)

Rest. If you work with a population that is chronically fatigued, consider offering an extended rest time, up to 10 minutes. If your setting is very goal driven, you may have to assuage some guilt, but know that rest for the weary is sometimes the greatest gift you can offer. If your children fall asleep, gently rouse them to wakefulness by touching a shoulder and using a quiet voice. Transition them back slowly with validating feedback (e.g., "You were very tired; look how you woke up and became alert again").

Centering/Close. The essentials of centering for alert at the end of the session are reorienting to the end of practice and expectations going forward, and holding onto any alert awareness that may have been learned. Follow the routines already established, take alert breaths with the breathing ball, and sing or recite the Alert song at the end.

Teaching and Using Alert at Home

Recommended Essentials
for Alert at Home

Rousing the body—breaths, quick energizing movements
Clear thoughts as a practice
Protecting the physical and emotional rest of your family

The alert concepts augmenting respect and calm continue to strengthen your efforts as a parent to raise children who have energy and willingness to perform tasks, even and especially "chores." It has always been beneficial, since the beginning of our race, to include young people in the work of the family, and alertness enhances a child's ability to do so, as well as your ability as a parent to facilitate that learning. It is healthy and appropriate to expect your children to share all these aspects of family life.

The quick movements and breaths that can be encouraged in a moment can aid in changing tired, grumpy energy, and can empower you to expect the possibility of change and cooperation. The message that thoughts can also aid in change, even if cajoling is necessary, can also support your efforts. An alert breath as that room needs to be cleaned, an alert frog on the way to the kitchen to set the table, and a list of clear thoughts posted by the homework table can all become part of your home.

Fatigue (both physical and emotional) is a chronic stressor for many families due to demanding schedules, overstimulation, screen time, poor diets, school and sport performance pressures—to name a few. Besides the well-recognized eight or more hours of sleep children's bodies need, emotional rest when our hearts and minds are not taxed is also critical. Although not always culturally supported, if your child is tired or weary, the first step is ensuring and protecting their rest at home, which may require taking a stand, saying "no" and turning out the lights. You will be rewarded over time with a child who wakes up refreshed and is naturally alert.

Chapter FIVE
Learning Time

This chapter begins the three final conceptual chapters regarding instruction about "times" of the day. Many mindfulness and yoga programs highlight the need for skill-building during transitions, but my observational inquiries led me to conclude that children also needed help understanding other times of the day. In a school setting, those times naturally emerged as learning, transition, and social times, but feedback from those in other settings including home have affirmed their usefulness to many settings. Although there is some overlap between expectations for learning, transition, and social times, establishing distinct understandings of the kind of times in a day, and explicit instruction for those times, has allowed children to be more skillful and helped the adults that serve them to be clearer. The times of day instruction has created conceptual "file folders" for children that act as a reference for skills (e.g., "Oh, it is _____ time. I need to _____.").

Learning time, our first area for consideration, is defined as a time when someone is teaching something and children are expected to learn, work on a task, or practice something, often involving effort. Learning times can be found in school settings, in sports, at extracurricular activities, at church, at home—it is a remarkable fact of childhood that children so often find themselves expected to learn something. Of course there are thousands of ways children learn and experience learning, but *Calm and Alert* focuses on those more structured learning times and strengthening a child's understanding of *how* to learn in those environments. Consequently, the definition includes the teaching that there is an expectation (called a "job" for explicit instruction) of some kind to do and that there are "skills" (listening, focus and following directions) that can be utilized with body, mind, and breath to make the job easier. It has grown out of my concern for the number of children who struggle, in body and mind, with the challenges of expectations in structured learning environments that require effort.

Modern life has allowed some children more freedom to avoid non-preferred tasks that require effort. Though this is a gift in light of history, there can be a danger for young people if they are thoroughly protected from every task that requires effort, the listening and focus needed for formal learning, or the discipline of following directions when appropriate. **It is actually a greater gift to teach children to respect any teacher—a person who wants to offer you some learning—by accepting the inevitability of doing tasks that require effort, practice to master, or may be repetitious, unpleasant, or not preferred.** Without this teaching and practice, children can develop habits of work avoidance, helplessness, dependence, and negative mind states (complaining, excuses) rather than the strength needed for sustained effort and skill development. To acquire positive traits for this kind of work is a gift for a lifetime.

With the foundation of respect, calm, and alert skills, children are more ready to learn the times of day concepts, starting with learning times. With respect for the teacher/student relationship well practiced, you can begin to teach children that learning can be an enjoyable partnership: A teacher, coach, leader, therapist, or parent wants to offer their knowledge, and children can be fully engaged with the teaching, learn, and then practice. With the developing awareness of the calm and alert states, children are more capable of listening, focusing, and understanding the how and why of directions so they will want to follow them. This is commonly known as being "ready to learn."

In approaching the skills of listening and focus two truths must be held. **First, the young brains of children in the areas of attention are still developing:** They tire when too many demands are placed on them without rest, and are taxed by hosts of internal and external distractions. **Second, culturally we expect more of children's attentional centers than in the past: higher performance in school, sports, and other activities, often not countered-balanced with activities that allow relaxation of those centers.** Consequently, my approach is to offer instruction in listening and focus to help the children better meet these demands (with kind understanding of the difficulties) that are developmentally digestible, explicit, and fun.

Similarly, the skill of following directions in structured learning environments is needed more than ever in a fast-paced, high-performing culture, but must be understood in the light of child development that has always known learning is process, not a race. The explicit instruction here teaches children about the partnership between a child and teacher, and the *how and why* of following directions for learning. A person imparting knowledge or skill enjoys sharing/teaching, a child follows the directions to engage with the teaching, and the experience can be pleasurable for all. Children can come to understand better that teachers create directions to steer learning, and children listen then act on the direction to actively engage in the partnership of learning. Without this skill, the process of learning can be discouraging for a child, rather than exciting and satisfying.

Learning Time Concepts

Learning Time:
Any time someone is teaching something;
any time a child is expected to learn,
work on a task, or practice something,
often involving effort.

Skills needed = listening, focus, following directions

Teaching Learning Time as a Class

Begin
Centering
Warm-up
Poses
Game
Rest
Centering/Close

Because learning times can be so various, I am offering two possible lessons in this chapter for flexibility and targeted focus. Although the three learning time skills taught are identical in the lessons, **Lesson 5a** emphasizes the development of strength in body and mind for the challenges that naturally arise during learning, while **Lesson 5b** offers a playful approach to sharpening the skills—particularly following directions. I regularly teach both these lessons consecutively. The material is rich enough to be broken down into small segments or taught over many sessions.

Lesson 5a: Learning Time, The Warrior

Begin. Now that the class routines are established, you can begin all ensuing classes reminding the children of the class flow and asking them if they remember what we do each week by picturing it as you give an overview. Say, "We start with the chime, then learn and sing a song, then move the tables, get out mats, roll them out and practice our poses, play our game, have rest time, and end. Can you picture it?" Proceed to explaining that our lesson today is about the first of three times of the day we will be learning about—learning time.

As you have your chime ready, ask, "What has the chime taught us so far?" hoping for the response "to listen" or "to be calm." Then say that the chime has more to teach us, this time about listening and focus. You have a number of choices here to develop awareness. You can offer the established chime practice, but add the explicit instruction that attention and focus are skills that can be practiced, and the chime practice can help us. When we listen as long as we can to the chime sound we are teaching our listening brain to be stronger. When we give all our attention to the three breaths we are teaching our attention centers of the brain to be stronger—and it is still helping us be calm and alert! You can also consider the following variations, designed to be taught consecutively, for continued instruction in attention and focus with the chime:

The Gazing Game

To develop awareness of attention,
and practice directing attention and focus.

1. **The Gazing Game 1:** Choose a focal point for the children to place their eyes/gaze. Keep the eyes relaxed and blink whenever needed. Ring the chime and challenge the children to keep their eyes on the focal point as long as the sound lasts. Praise them, have them relax their gaze, take three deep breaths, then have them gaze again for the final sound.

2. **The Gazing Game 2:** Have the children pick their own focal point and follow Gazing Game 1 guidelines.

3. **The Gazing Game 3:** First, explicitly teach the concept of a distraction, which I define as "anything that takes your attention away from the most important thing for learning." Distractions can be anything inside us or outside of us, and we can learn to ignore them to help us with learning. Tell the children we are going to play the Gazing Game, have them choose a focal point or offer one, and say, "I am going to try to distract you. See if you can ignore the distractions." Then ring the chime and make noise, cough or sneeze, run water, turn the lights off then on, etc. Praise them for their amazing abilities to ignore such distractions! Continue with Gazing Game 1 guidelines and expect giggles.

As you introduce the Learning Time song, define what a learning time is—tailored to your setting. If in a school, it is a time when teachers are teaching and kids are learning (ask them to name some); if at a sports practice, a time when the coach is teaching a skill and children are expected to practice, etc. Be playful as you teach the line "your number one job" by asking, "Did you know you *have* a job?" You can expand on this by saying, "Kids do have jobs—to learn. It is practice for when you become an adult." Name the three skills needed: listening, focus, and following directions. Then teach the song and sing or recite it, with or without hand signs.

Learning Time Song

It is learning time
It is learning time
My number one job
My number one job
Listening and focus
Following directions
Learning time
Learning time

Proceed with the beginning routines until all mats are out and children are sitting cross-legged in the center of mats ready for practice. (See Chapter 2 for establishing routines if you have not done so.)

Centering. Remind the children that we have now learned both calm and alert breaths, and both can help us at learning times. If we are tired, we can use alert breaths to be more awake; and if we are upset or over-excited, we can use our calm breaths to become steady. Now we will learn the book breath, which can be done as a calm breath or an alert breath—use your discretion to do one or both.

Book breath: Sit up straight and place index finger in the air. Breathe in to the count of three while moving finger horizontally to right. Breathe out to count of three, moving finger down toward floor. Breathe in to count of three, moving finger horizontally to left. Breathe out to count of three, moving finger up toward ceiling. This can also be done as an alert breath by making the same square shape with quick breathing.

Warm-up. As you introduce this warm-up, have your two small mason jars (one with mud, one with clear water) ready. Remind the children of the chant we learned earlier, particularly "my mind is my helper when it's ready to learn" and tap your head as you chant it (See Chapter 1). Then say, "Our mind makes words and pictures called thoughts. Some help our learning and some get in the way of learning and make things harder. Thoughts that help us are called clear (hold up jar with water). Thoughts that get in the way and make things harder are called muddy (hold up jar of mud). We can choose clear thoughts, which will help us learn more easily and be happier. Or we can choose muddy thoughts, which usually make learning harder and make us unhappy." Ask for examples of muddy or clear thoughts, or offer some:

Clear	**Muddy**
Yes	No
I like this	I hate this
I will try	I don't want to
I can do this	I can't do this

Offer compassion by mentioning that everybody has muddy thoughts sometimes and it can be hard to change them, especially when we are sad or mad. Then offer this warm-up as a way to change our thoughts to clear:

Washing Machine

Sit up straight with legs crossed. Think of some muddy thoughts you want to wash clean. Reach behind you and grab the muddy thought, then reach your arms up and over and pretend to put them in a washing machine in front of you. Close the lid. Sit up straight, bring your arms close to your chest, and twist side to side slowly like a washing machine. Say "Ding" when it is done. Open the lid, reach in, and pretend to shake out a shirt and name a clear thought. Reach behind you and put it in the dryer.

To do the dryer, sit up straight, breathe in and reach your arms up overhead. Then place your right hand on the floor by your right side and reach your left arm overhead. Breathe in, center, then repeat on the left side and go back and forth a few times. Say "Ding" when it is done. Reach in to the dryer and pull out the clean shirt. Breathe in and bring your hands up overhead; breathe out and bring your hands down to the sides of your body with a "yes breath."

Poses. For this lesson there is one pose and a poem offered, used to teach the message that you have to be strong and brave to learn new things and have clear thoughts. In introducing the warrior, I emphasize that they were strong and brave people of long ago, and try to minimize thoughts of battles and weapons.

Warrior: Start in mountain. Tap on one leg and step it forward without strain, bend knee. Other leg is straight behind. Raise arms, look forward, deep breath. Feel strong and brave.

While on the first side, have them bring their arms in front of their chests, ready to clap, and teach the first two lines of this poem:

> I am a warrior
> Strong and smart

Have them come back to mountain and repeat pose on other side, with clapping hands ready, and teach the second two lines:

> I have clear thoughts
> Right from the start

Back to mountain, clap, and recite entire poem.

Game. The game is a variation on "Stop" utilizing the warrior pose. The basics of the Stop game (we move, then we stop—safe and in control) are reviewed, assuming you have played before (see Chapter 2, Respect), then:

Stop Variation: The Rocking Warrior

Have child/children stand like a mountain at the back of their mats, tap one leg, and come into warrior pose on one side, encouraging them to feel their strength and steadiness.

Model for them how to do the "tricky switch" of hopping up and switching to warrior on the other side. Then have them practice. Be sure their stances are not wider than a few feet apart for safety.

Then model the rocking warrior: in warrior stance rock up and back, putting weight on the front, then the back leg; then have them practice.

To play the game, say "go" and have the children do the rocking warrior. Say "stop" and have them stop. Say "tricky switch" and have them switch to warrior on the other side, then repeat. If this is difficult for anyone, offer the option of coming to the back of their mats and switching from here. Using music (rock while music plays; stop when music stops) can be an enhancement.

Rest. In this rest time, if you feel the learning about being still has been well-established while laying on backs, you can offer other options for laying comfortably, such as side or belly. If you do, remind the children that we continue to find stillness in any position. Return to the familiar garden, and highlight that when we work hard at learning, it is healthy to then have a rest.

Rest Time Script: The Garden

"Lay on your back and become still on your mat by using your deep calm breaths. Notice your feet, legs, torso, arms, hands, neck, and head and become still. This is how we rest our bodies. Can you feel quiet and steady?

Now we will rest our minds and heart with a story:

Picture a beautiful blue sky and the sun shining down on you. Imagine a big field and see yourself walk, skip, run, or hop through the field. You hear, then see, a steady stream and walk beside it. The bubbling sounds seem to say 'lay all your cares in my waters' and you take any cares you have and imagine them washed away by the stream. You keep walking until you reach the gate of a beautiful garden.

See yourself push open the gate and step inside. Look around the garden, notice birds and butterflies, flowers and trees; feel the warm breeze on your cheek. Let the beauty and sounds remind you of a quiet, steady place you have inside you. Notice a table with healthy foods like fruits and vegetables, and clear water, and imagine eating and drinking with someone who cares about you."

Pause here and allow silence for a few minutes.

"Now we must say goodbye to your beautiful place, but we never have to leave our quiet, steady place—it is always with you. Walk back through the field to _____ (their present setting). Turn on your side and pause there. Bring your knees into your chest, wrap your arms around your knees and give yourself a hug and whisper 'I am calm.' Now push yourself up to sitting."

Centering/Close. Continue reinforcing the established routines of sitting cross-legged and straight as we close our practice. Remind them of the book breath we learned and ask, "How are you feeling and what kind of breath do you need right now, calm or alert? Choose the breath that is right for you." Then lead then in the book breath, letting them choose a calm or alert version. This helps develop self-awareness and the generalization of the breath practices, based on need.

Follow the established routines for rolling up mats, storing them, and restoring the room. Praise them at every step until they are finally sitting like a mountain in their seats. Sing/recite the Learning Time song. After you say, "I respect you," and hear the children say, "I respect you," mention that every time they listened, focused, and followed directions, they gave you as the teacher a flower of respect. Thank them for that gift.

Calm and Alert Lesson: Learning Time

Lesson 5a

Grade/Group_____   Date_____

Materials needed:
Chime
Clear and muddy jars

Lesson

Begin:
Learning Time song

Centering:
The book breath: calm or alert

Warm-up:
Washing Machine

Poses:
Warrior
Warrior poem:

I am a warrior
Strong and smart
I have clear thoughts
Right from the start

Game:
Stop variation: Rocking Warrior

Rest:
Garden

Centering/Close:
The book breaths
Learning Time song

Lesson 5b: Learning Time, The Dogs

Begin. Now that the class routines are established, you can begin all ensuing classes reminding the children of the class flow and asking them if they remember what we do each week by picturing it as you give an overview. Say, "We start with the chime, then learn and sing a song, then move the tables, get out mats, roll them out and practice our poses, play our game, have rest time, and end. Can you picture it?" Proceed to explaining that our lesson today is about the first of three times of the day we will be learning about—learning time. If you have taught Lesson 5a, offer the regular chime practice, or see Lesson 5a for the Gazing Game variations. Then sing/recite the Learning Time song.

Learning Time Song

It is learning time
It is learning time
My number one job
My number one job
Listening and focus
Following directions
Learning time
Learning time

Tell the class we will be having fun today pretending to be and doing many dog poses and it will help us understand how following directions helps us learn. Teachers ask us to follow directions because it steers us toward the learning they hope for us. When we can follow directions quickly, we engage with the teacher like a partner. To enhance this, say, "We can follow directions: **The minute he/ she says it, exactly as he/she says it.**" Clap your hands as you say this. Have the children repeat and clap. If they enjoy this, clap and say this throughout the lesson when you see them following directions in a timely fashion.

Centering. As you introduce the doggie breath, say that when it is a learning time and we have to follow directions, it is helpful to be alert so you will hear the directions and know what to do. After they do the doggie breath, ask, "Are you alert?"

> **Doggie breath:** Sit up straight like a sitting mountain and breathe in two breaths in succession while wiggling nose; exhale a long slow breath.

Warm-up. Review the teaching about clear and muddy thoughts and hold up the jars: Clear thoughts help us with learning, muddy thoughts get in the way of learning. (See Lesson 5a for full instruction.) Tell the children that to learn all the dog poses, you are hoping to teach, we will want to practice the clear thoughts: "I am listening/I am focused/I follow directions." You can have them repeat after you as you say them. You may also want to show them what muddy thoughts can do: Name a muddy thought such as "I don't want to" or "no I won't" and look unhappy and grumpy; then point to your head and model changing to clear thoughts "I want to," "yes," and smiling alertly. Yes, some children need such explicit instruction in this area!

Now you are ready for these dog warm-ups, the first four in the dog flow:

Dog Warm-up

Calm sitting dog: Exactly like sitting mountain—legs folded under with bottom resting on feet, sitting straight on floor.

Calm standing dog (sometimes known as "table"): Coming to hands and knees with hands under shoulders, knees under feet, straight back.

Arching/bowing dog:
From calm standing dog,
breathe out and arch the
back, breathe in and bow
the back.

Tail-wagging dog: Starting on hands and knees, imagine you
have a tail. Breathe in, center, then curve to the right as you
exhale and look for your tail. Breathe in, back to center; breathe
out, curve to left. Go back and forth steadily, "not too fast, not
too slow."

Poses. Offered here are the remaining six dogs in the flow. Tell the class that if
everyone is following directions quickly, we should be able to learn all the dogs
today; and then celebrate how many they are able to learn as you go. You can
also go back and forth between the different dogs as you teach them, such as
returning to puppy dog for rest after exertion. Throughout, ask, "Who is having
a clear thought?" and praise them for their hard work and practice.

Dog Flow

Puppy dog: Come into puddle ("child's"
pose), but keep arms outstretched
in front.

Twisty dog (also known as "thread the needle"): Start on hands
and knees. Lift up right hand toward ceiling with a breath in;
breathe out and bring right hand down under torso and behind
the left arm. Bottom stays in air, knees firm on ground, right
shoulder rests on mat. Repeat on other side.

Up dog: Start on hands and knees; bring hands a few inches toward the front of mat. Breathe in, arch back so that the face is turned up to ceiling, front of legs flattened on mat and the entire body is one long arch upward. For a greater challenge, come up onto toes.

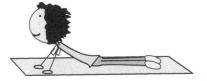

Down dog: Start in calm standing dog, on hands and knees. Curl toes and raise hip area toward ceiling until body is in shape of a "V." Straighten legs and arms, head between forearms.

Resting dog: Lay on back, legs outstretched, arms at sides, relaxed.

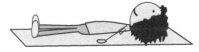

Frozen dog: From resting dog, bring straight arms and straight legs toward ceiling and be frozen. Back is flat.

Happy dog (also known as "happy baby"): Lay on back in resting dog. Hug knees to chest, arms wrapped around legs. Grab outer edge of right foot with right hand, left foot with left hand. With back flat, spread feet out and up toward ceiling and rock back and forth.

Game. This game is another variation on the Stop game that is a way of illustrating to the children what they have successfully learned due to their skill practice, and also helps you see what they have internalized.

Stop Variation: Favorite Dog

Have all the children start on hands and knees in "calm standing dog." Tell them that when you say "go" they will be tail-wagging dogs, and when you say "stop" they will stop/ freeze. Then you will say "favorite dog" and they can pick their favorite dog to do. (You may want to review all the dogs we have learned today.) Then say "puppy dog" and have everyone rest. Repeat or end. If you repeat and you want to avoid repetition, say "different favorite dog" to encourage other choices. Praise them for steadiness, safety, and control. Celebrate all the various dogs you see. End with puppy dog.

Rest. In this rest time, if you feel the learning about being still has been well-established while laying on backs, you can offer other options for laying comfortably, such as side or belly. If you do, remind the children that we continue to find stillness in any position. If the group is still unsteady, have them lay in "resting dog" to continue the theme.

Centering/Close. Continue reinforcing the established routines of sitting cross-legged and straight as we close our practice. Remind them of all the calm and alert breaths we have learned and ask, "How are you feeling and what kind of breath do you need right now, calm or alert? Choose the breath that is right for you." If taught in the last lesson, lead them in the book breath, letting them choose a calm or alert version, or other breaths. This helps develop self-awareness and the generalization of the breath practices, based on need.

Follow the established routines for rolling up mats, storing them, and restoring the room. Praise them at every step, until they are finally sitting like a mountain in their seats. Sing/recite the Learning Time song. After you say, "I respect you," and hear the children say, "I respect you," mention that every time they followed directions and learned what you hoped to teach them, they gave you as the teacher a flower of respect. Thank them for that gift.

Rest Time Script: The Cozy House

"Lay on your back and become still on your mat by using your deep, calm breaths. Notice your feet, legs, torso, arms, hands, neck, and head and become still. This is how we rest our bodies.

Now we will rest our minds and heart with a story:

Picture a beautiful blue sky and the sun shining down on you. Imagine a big field and see yourself walk, skip, run, or hop through the field. You hear, then see, a steady stream and walk beside it. The bubbling sounds seem to say 'lay all your cares in my waters' and you take any cares you have and imagine them washed away by the stream. See yourself walking up a path until you reach a cozy house.

See yourself step into this place, and as you do feel any cares you may have leaving your mind, leaving a clearness. Look around the cozy house. See comfortable chairs, a soft cushion on the floor, a warm fire in the fireplace. Picture people that care about you there, smiling at you. Let the beauty and sounds remind you of a quiet, steady place you have inside you."

Pause here and allow silence for a few minutes.

"Now it is time to say goodbye to your beautiful place, but we never have to leave our quiet, steady place—it is always with you. Walk back through the field to _____ (their present setting). Turn on your side and pause there. Bring your knees into your chest, wrap your arms around your knees and give yourself a hug. Now push yourself up to sitting."

Calm and Alert Lesson: Learning Time

Lesson 5b

Grade/Group_____   Date_____

Materials needed:
Chime
Clear and muddy jars

Lesson

Begin:
Learning Time song

Centering:
The doggy breath

Warm-up:
Calm sitting dog, calm standing dog,
arching dog, bowing dog, tail-wagging dog

Poses:
Dog flow

Game:
Stop variation: Favorite Dog

Rest:
Cozy House

Centering/Close:
Pick a breath right for you
Learning Time song

Teaching and Using Learning Time in Other Settings

As you enter into the three times of the day concepts, beginning here with learning time, consideration of your goals with your particular population is critical. What kind of learning are your children expected to do in your setting? This question will lead you to utilize just one or all of the essentials, or particular elements of the class lessons that can highlight and explicitly teach the skills your children most need.

Recommended Essentials

You can be a learner by using your body and mind, and partnering with your teacher
Listening, focus, and following directions can improve
Choosing clear versus muddy thoughts
Rest after exertion

For some children with special needs, establishing the first essential "you can be a learner" is foundational. It is established by the explicit teaching of the word "learner," the continual practices with the body, mind, and breath, and encouraging the understanding of the role of the teacher. The three skills needed for learning—listening, focus, and following directions—might seem almost unattainable for children with attention/EF issues, cognitive impairments, or severe behavioral challenges, and they can become disheartened about the possibility of improvement. But even if it is evident only in moments of practice at first, improvement is possible and celebrating incremental gains can give children some hope for themselves as learners. These first two essentials, as one special needs boy I helped said, "taught me *how* to learn."

The clear and muddy thought concepts have been very popular with my challenged children, perhaps because they have too much firsthand experience with mind barriers such as discouragement or negative self-talk. Changing a thought is a simple message, can be concretely practiced, and any child can experience some small benefit from the practice.

Finally, offering your population rest throughout the process of learning validates the reality that they work harder than most and understandably fatigue more easily. Expect exertion, then kindly offer small rests as you go.

Modifying Class Elements

Because two lessons are offered in this chapter, the modifications here will highlight the best of both for teaching the essentials.

Begin.   Continue to build on all the particular routines you may have established for your setting, remembering you are hoping to teach the children a rhythm for the start of practice. If the chime has worked thus far, ring it once to begin, and say, "The chime is going to teach us more about learning today." If you want to simplify the message, say, "You are a learner who can listen and focus. Let's practice," and do the chime practice as established. If that goes well, play the Gazing Game 1, and consider using a large colored circle, a favorite toy/ preferred object, or you as the focal point:

The Gazing Game 1: Chose a focal point for the children to place their eyes/gaze. Keep the eyes relaxed and blink whenever needed. Ring the chime and challenge the children to keep their eyes on the focal point as long as the sound lasts. Praise them, have them relax their gaze, take three deep breaths, then have them gaze again for the final sound.

Take any liberty appropriate with the words to the song/poem to match your setting. Be over-the-top explicit by saying, "Right now is a learning time," "I am your teacher for learning," "This is your job," as you begin.

Centering.   Always be sure everyone is as settled and steady as possible here, utilizing the straight spine, the sitting bones instruction, and the calm breaths as the baseline. Teaching the book breath is more grounding for calming; the doggie breath more exciting for those that need alerting. The essential message is "using your breath can help you learn."

Warm-up. For enhanced, very explicit instruction in clear/muddy thoughts, have the jars ready, as well as happy and sad/mad feeling pictures. Hold up the clear jar near your brain and the happy picture and say, "You have words and pictures in your brain. Clear thoughts make us happy, and make learning easy." Then say a clear thought such as "I like this" or "I can do this" while smiling and have the children repeat it if they can. Then hold up the muddy jar near your brain and the sad/mad picture and say, "Muddy thoughts make us grumpy and make learning hard." Then say a muddy thought such as "I don't want to do this" or "no" and make a grumpy face. Say, "We can change our muddy thoughts to clear," and put the muddy jar away, keeping the clear jar visible. Then use the Washing Machine warm-up as described earlier.

If you want to focus just on the three learning time skills, spend time here teaching that your ears help you listen (have them tug their ears), your eyes help you focus (have them tap the outside of their eyes), and when a teacher asks you to do something, your ears and eyes are open, and then you do it. This helps learning. Then jump right to the doggie breath, and the calm sitting and calm standing dogs. As you do them, repeatedly bring their attention to how they are listening, how they are looking at you, how they are doing what you asked them to do, which is following directions.

Poses. Choose between the warrior or the other dogs, depending on the direction you want to take the lesson. (Physically modify the warrior by keeping the stance narrow.) Throughout, bring their attention to clear thoughts and how they help us, and all they can learn when they listen, focus, and follow directions. If your population tires easily, praise them for anything they can do, and regularly go to the puddle or puppy dog poses with the message "we are taking a little rest after our hard work." Continue to point out that they are learning and what they are learning.

Game. If the warrior or dog variations of the Stop game are too complex, offer the basic Stop game and highlight their ability to follow the direction "stop" by listening to the word and doing it with their bodies. If they get over-excited by the dogs, rather than "favorite dog" after they stop, name a dog, and stick with calm sitting dog, calm standing dog, puppy dog, and frozen dog for steadiness.

Rest. Consider offering a few extra minutes of rest this session because the lesson is more demanding. You may also want to add some affirmations once they have reached the beautiful place such as "I am proud of myself," "I used my clear thoughts," or "I worked hard today," to name a few.

Centering/Close. If your population is still learning the calm and alert breaths, just offer one of each and bring their awareness to how they are feeling. Otherwise, let them choose, as explained in the lesson previously. If there is time when working with individuals or small groups, consider asking one of the following questions before leaving the mats:

- When were you most focused today?

- When were you the best listener?

- When did you follow directions?

- What was the most fun learning today?

Restore the room, and finish with the song and the statement: "This was a learning time, and you were a learner."

Teaching and Using Learning Time at Home

Recommended Essentials

Choosing clear versus muddy thoughts
Practicing how to listen, focus, and follow directions
Feeling satisfaction after effort
Confidence: feeling strong and smart

As a parent, you may be unused to calling home experiences learning times because the learning is less structured, more various, more open and free, and it is wonderful that home is this way! Consider this concept an offering for those times when structure and skill is needed and useful for a task at hand. The vocabulary and expectations could be a support to your parenting as you approach teaching your child safety rules, the appropriate use of tools, doing chores well, or doing manual tasks, to name a few. All of these tasks optimally require skill development, effort, and positive attitudes such as respect for you as you teach, and the task at hand. What children learn from you at home about expectations creates their foundation for a lifetime of learning.

The first essential for such learning times in the home is choosing clear versus muddy thoughts, which is the foundation for facing experiences with a positive attitude, particularly difficult ones. As always, you are the first role model and your child is watching how you approach new tasks, chores, and work. It requires some strength of will and calm positivity as a parent to offer kindness about facing difficulties, with the expectation that your child will put forth the effort needed. Though it is tempting to avoid teaching them this "change muddy thoughts to clear" skill by giving in/up when children complain, refuse, or tantrum about non-preferred activities, their suffering will be even greater as they enter the world and are required to learn so many things without this strength, from others besides the people who love them best.

The second essential you can offer is practice in how to listen, focus, and follow directions—just three of the many skills needed for learning. The modern age offers much instruction in distraction, disconnection, and putting forth minimal effort, so it is a bold step to offer the opposite. Establishing a home in which family members authentically listen to one another and respect what they hear teaches the *how* of listening. Offering a child an environment with undistracted time to engage in real-time activities that require effort such as expressive art, nature walks, or making things allows the development of various types of focus. Establishing early that certain directions at home are essential for learning without undue protests will teach them an easy internal "yes" toward unavoidable, expected tasks learning sometimes requires. These foundations, when learned in your home, will help your child in every structured learning environment they encounter.

The last two essentials are fruits that come to young people who have developed the "muscle" of using clear thoughts, listening, focus, and following directions during times of learning. Lasting satisfaction is only truly learned when some effort is required, challenge is faced clearly, work is completed. Confidence only grows and flowers in children who have had many experiences of partnering with supportive adults, practicing, working hard, and endeavoring to learn something new.

Chapter SIX

Transition Time

Transition Time Song

It's transition time
It's transition time
Time for change
Time for change
Mountain, cloud, and eagle
Steady, careful, focused
Transition time
Transition time

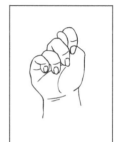

Transition times, our second time of the day for consideration and skill building, are a well-known challenge for anyone who helps children maneuver through them smoothly. Transition times are times when things change: an in-between time when we go from one thing to another. There are many, many daily transition times in the life of a modern child: waking up; getting ready in the morning; going to and leaving school, daycare, or other activities; in between subjects and during a subject in school; mealtimes; going from indoors to outdoors—to name a few! Broadening the scope, transition times can also refer to seasonal changes, the rhythm of a school year, and an array of family and other changes that may involve loss.

In my inquiries, transition times are vulnerable times for many children because there may be confusion about expectations, adult attention may wane for a bit, children have a tendency to relax their self-control, activity levels can be chaotically high, and the change at hand may not be welcome. Consequently, transition times require skillful steadiness, care, focus, and flexibility to be smooth, quick, and as easy as possible. The power of self-regulation is most evident here because the child with such an inner compass to rely on for the needed skills can maintain themselves while things around them change. Children with lagging skills in self-regulation are more likely to struggle and experience stress at transition times.

Traditionally, a skilled adult sensitive to these challenges will provide a high level of structure during transitions times, especially for young children. The calm and alert skills for transition time (steady, careful, focused) build and expand on the previously taught skills for self-regulation and social awareness, to be practiced when they are needed most. Self-regulated children who can monitor their own bodies and minds, choosing to be steady, can discover their ability to partner with adults and peers to make transitions, individually and in a group, much more manageable. This partnership allows everyone to relax into a confidence that the transition will be smooth because each individual is doing their part through self-regulation.

The foundational skills of respect, calm, and alert continue to be reviewed, practiced, and expanded in this chapter. The practice of respect offers transition times a self-awareness regarding others and space, and the "seriousness" needed to avoid the temptation to become overly silly and lose focus. A return to the foundational steadiness learned from the calm breaths and skills is emphasized, with additional instruction about the effects of being what I call "windy" (taught as the opposite of steady) during transition times. Being alert continues to be a valuable tool for paying attention to what is required during a transition and staying focused until the transition is over.

The learning time skills offered in the previous chapter are built upon, particularly because there are often multiple tasks required (pick up, gather this, go here, remember this, etc.) that listening and following directions can only aid. The mindset skills, particularly the practice of focus and clear thoughts, become critical for smooth transition times. Transitions create a great deal of energy and motion, and it is very easy for children to lose focus, whether it be the focus of picking up, preparing for a new task, or getting in the car at the end of a gathering. The focal point comes to be the end of the transition, and can be taught and practiced. Clear thoughts are helpful for the flexibility transitions require, particularly those that are unwelcome and non-preferred.

Thoughts such as "oh well," "no big deal," and "OK" rather than "no" lead to more cooperation and partnership with adults mentioned earlier. Transition times are unavoidable, but the chaos, stress, and distress can be greatly reduced by self-management—the seed of resilience for a lifetime.

Transition Time Concepts

Transition Time:
A time of change;
an in-between time when we go
from one thing to another

Skills needed = steady, careful, focused

Teaching Transition Time as a Class

Begin
Centering
Warm-up
Poses
Game
Rest
Centering/Close

Lesson 6: Transition Time

Begin. By this time in the lesson series, the group you are teaching hopefully has a memory and internal framework concerning the structure and rhythm of the lessons. As a teacher, this allows you to bring the light of your attention specifically on the transition times in the class and all the instruction-rich opportunities as transitions occur. It never hurts, though, to begin by reminding the children, "We start with the chime, then learn and sing a song, then move the tables, get out mats, roll them out and practice our poses, play our game, have rest time, and end. Can you picture it?" as suggested in the last chapter.

Begin this lesson reminding the children that last week we started learning about the times of the day. You can ask, "Does anyone remember the name of the time of day we learned last time?" (or simply tell them). Then mention that today we will be learning more about the second kind of time of the day—transition times. (With very young children, have them repeat the word.) Define transition time as a time of change when we go from one thing to another. I like to assist this teaching with this clapping gesture:

Rest your right palm on top of the outstretched left palm, toward the left side of the body. As you say "one thing" flip outstretched hands over to the right side with a clap. As you say "to another" flip outstretched hands over to the left side. Have children repeat it with you.

Then say, "There are lots and lots of transition times in a day, and during our *Calm and Alert* class. Can anyone name one?" The children are well served if you continue to name each transition time throughout the lesson.

In this lesson, I would sing the song/recite the poem before the chime practice, utilizing the ASL sign for change. This will enhance the focus on the three skills through the chime practice:

Transition Time Song

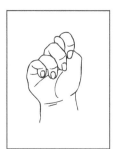

It's transition time
It's transition time
Time for change
Time for change
Mountain, cloud, and eagle
Steady, careful, focused
Transition time
Transition time

Proceed to the chime practice, mentioning that it is helpful to be calm and steady when things change. Pause for a moment as the practice ends and bring their attention to their feeling of steadiness.

Chime Practice

Ring chime, listen as long as you can
Lead children in 3–5 slow, deep breaths
Ring chime, listen as long as you can

One final quick teaching point here before you move to preparing the room for practice: remain steady, not windy, during times of change. Tell the children we are about to have our first transition in our lesson today and that sometimes during transition times people become windy instead of steady, careful, and focused. Have the children put their hands on their belly and feel their steadiness, then have them do the wind:

Wind: Start in sitting mountain, keeping sitting bones firmly on ground. Lift arms up in air and sway upper arms and torso back and forth while making a windy sound with mouth. Used to illustrate the opposite of steady.

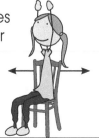

If time allows, model what windiness can look like in the *Calm and Alert* class—pretend to be a child and wander from the area, or pick up a rolled-up mat loosely so it unravels, or wander around with a mat without finding a spot (variations are endless!). I have found that using the word "windy" has allowed adults to offer a non-judgmental term for dysregulation, and has enhanced the ability of teachers to give corrective feedback with compassion.

As the class then transitions, give frequent praise to children who are steady, not windy. Keep reminding them that their focus is to finally be sitting on their mats.

Centering. Continue noticing all aspects of the transition as children settle onto sitting on their mats. To keep awareness high, consider using your chime by saying, "Can our transitions be over by the end of (3,4,5) chime sounds?" and then ring the chime and name what number chime sound we are experiencing. In between, praise the children who are finished transitioning, with the teaching that every individual who is steady helps the transition be over. When everyone is settled, point out that the transition is over and we are ready for our breath practice.

The breath for today is a calm breath to underscore how helpful being calm is during transition times:

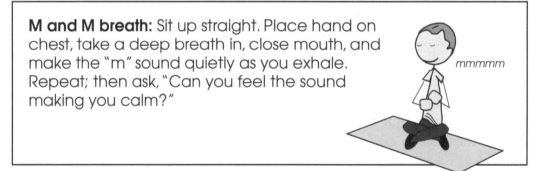

M and M breath: Sit up straight. Place hand on chest, take a deep breath in, close mouth, and make the "m" sound quietly as you exhale. Repeat; then ask, "Can you feel the sound making you calm?"

mmmmm

Warm-up. The warm-up today requires the body transition frequently, which is rich material for the theme, but use with discretion if your group is generally windy or has not had the practice of previous lessons. The Boat warm-up is a steady alternative to Blast Off. As you start, mention that our bodies will be moving and changing as we do Blast Off, and we will be practicing being steady, careful, and focused.

Blast Off

Sit on your mat with your feet flat in front of you, knees bent. Place your hands behind your trunk: feel steady here. Breathe out slowly and bring the knees down to the right. Breathe in, bring knees back up. Breathe out and bring them over to the left. Go back and forth two times. This movement will be the countdown for the blast off—starting with10 and knees to right, nine with knees to left, back and forth slowly until zero.

For blast off: Knees stay to the right as you push up onto your knees with your right hand near your right hip for support and your left hand swinging up and over to right. Then slowly come down and swing knees to left for blast off on the left side. Come up onto left knees, your left hand near your hip for support, your right arm swinging up and over to left.

Another teaching point when this warm-up gets lively is that if we feel ourselves getting windy, we can always *become* steady by sitting back down on our mats, or taking a calm breath.

Poses. Introduce the eagle flow while the children are still sitting. Say that eagles are mighty birds that have excellent eyes for focusing and hunting, and use their wings skillfully in the wind. Build excitement that we will now become eagles. Then proceed through each of the eagles. The following game requires the children know at least the perching, flapping, and soaring eagles.

Eagle Series

Baby eagle: Squat with knees together, hands resting on mat on each side. Breathe.

Eagle stretching wings: From baby eagle, slowly bring arms out to sides as wings. As you breathe in, slowly come to standing and bring arms up overhead until wrists touch. With the exhale, bring arms back to sides.

Perching eagle: Tuck hands into armpits, elbows bent and tucked close to sides. Look from one side to the other. While they perch, the teacher can "be the wind" by moving around the room while waving arms and making windy sounds, saying: "Can you stay steady on your perch as the wind blows around you?"

Flapping eagle: Starting in mountain, bring arms out wide and up with an in-breath, down with an out-breath. Repeat slowly with calm breaths or quickly with alert breaths, a few at a time only.

Soaring eagle: Starting in mountain, bring arms out to a "T" position. With torso remaining straight, breathe in and center; then as you breathe out, tilt torso to right. Repeat on other side, rhythmically going back and forth.

Hunting eagle: Starting in perching eagle, look down in front of toes and imagine there is a mouse you want to catch. Breathe in and bring arms up and overhead until wrists touch, then swoop down steadily and grab your mouse. Return to standing and gobble it up!

Game. Have the children sit like a mountain while you teach the concept of flexibility and introduce the Switcheroo game, which requires a higher level of self-regulation than in previous games. Have a piece of clay large enough for the class to see, a pencil, and the muddy and clear jars ready. Tell the group we will be playing a game called "Switcheroo" in a minute that requires we be steady, careful, and focused like we have been practicing. Say, "There will be a lot of changes in the game: the way we move, where we go, and sharing our mats with others. Another skill that can help us is called flexibility. Flexibility is when we are able to change easily like a piece of clay" *(hold up clay)* "and have clear thoughts" *(hold up jar)* "to help us change. Being like clay means we can move and change" *(move clay in different ways)* "and think clearly with thoughts such as: 'Oh well, that's okay. This is a small problem; no big deal.' The opposite is being like a pencil" *(hold up pencil)* "that cannot bend or change" *(try to bend it and show that it cannot without breaking).* "Usually we have muddy thoughts when we are like a pencil" *(hold up jar)* "such as: 'I don't want to.' 'No.' or 'This is a big problem.' Let's be like clay as we play."

Being like clay	**Being like a pencil**
Clear thoughts	*Muddy thoughts*
Oh, well	I don't want to
That's okay	This is not okay with me
This is a small problem	This is a giant problem
No big deal	This is a big deal

Switcheroo: Eagle

Have child/children stand like a mountain in the middle of the mat or space. Mention that the name of the game "switcheroo" is a funny word for "change." Put on lively music and give an instruction to move: either a soaring or flapping eagle (pick one). When the music stops, children stop and become a perching eagle. You then say, "Switcheroo _____ (1,2,3,4,5)" and children move to share a mat with that many people as perching eagles.

Play music again and start a new round, each time giving a new number to the switcheroo. Have the child/children smile if they feel safe and respected. With much practice, you can put a blanket down and have a class of 25 self-regulated students fit on one space.

Throughout the game point out children who are being steady, careful, focused, and flexible. Make special note of anyone who was flexible like clay: moving to another mat, inviting people to their mat, solving any problem. If you have a very regulated group that is handling the game well, do not miss any opportunity to celebrate the beauty of the movements—a sky full of majestic eagles. For the last round (if all has gone well) have them return to *any* mat with clear thoughts, standing like a mountain.

Rest. Due to the fact that this lesson offers so much practice in transitions, take extra time here to guide the group to become steady in mountain, find the gentle rain, and rest in puddle while taking long, deep breaths. Say, "We have had a lot of transitions, but rest time is a time when we become still and rest from change." Building on options from the last lesson about finding a comfortable way to rest, ask them to notice the feeling of now being still.

Rest Time Script: The Mountain Eagle

"Now that we are resting our bodies by being still, we will rest our hearts and minds with a rest time story.

Picture a beautiful blue sky and the sun shining down on you, feel the sun shining on a steady place inside you. Imagine a big field and see yourself walk, skip, run, or hop through the field. You hear, then see, a quiet, steady stream and walk beside it. The bubbling sounds seem to say 'lay all your cares in my waters.' You reach down and touch the water and imagine your cares washed away by the stream. The stream takes you to the foot of a beautiful mountain.

You look up at the mountain and become an eagle. See yourself flying up, up, up to the top of the mountain, then perch on the top of a high tree. Look around: See other eagles soaring and perching near you, other mountains in the distance; feel the wind, the sun shining on you. Notice the quiet, steady place inside you. The place that never changes, and is always with you."

Pause here and allow silence for a few minutes.

"Now it is time to say goodbye. Imagine soaring down the side of the beautiful mountain, but we never have to leave our quiet, steady place—it is always with you. As you land at the base of the mountain, imagine becoming a person again, and walk back through the field to _____ (their present setting). Turn on your side and pause there. Bring your knees into your chest, wrap your arms around your knees and give yourself a hug. Feel proud that you have been so steady through every transition. Now push yourself up to sitting."

Centering/Close. Once sitting again, guide the group in a few "M and M" breaths, perhaps utilizing the breathing ball to ensure the breath is slow and deep. Remind the children that it is beneficial to be calm in order to help the upcoming transition be steady, careful, and focused. With your words, walk them through the process by saying, "Our transition starts as we come to the back of our mats, roll them up, sit like a little mountain, and ask 'Am I steady?' It continues as we get up, walk to the mat bin, return our mats, walk back into the room, ask 'Is it safe?' then move the tables and sit down. The transition is over when we are all back in our seats." When everyone is seated, celebrate their steadiness, care and focus, and how we worked together to make the transition smooth. End with the Transition Time song.

Calm and Alert Lesson: Transition Time

Lesson 6

Grade/Group_____   Date_____

Materials needed:
Clay/pencil
Clear/muddy jars

<u>Lesson</u>

Begin:
Transition Time song

Centering:
M and M breath

Warm-up:
Blast Off

Poses:
Eagle flow

Game:
Teach flexibility
Switcheroo, with eagle movements

Rest:
Mountain, with eagle

Centering/Close:
M and M breath or other calm breath
Transition Time song

Teaching and Using Transition Time in Other Settings

Consideration and kindness should be our starting place as we explore transition times for special populations, who find regulation and social skills so difficult and struggle mightily with change. Like me, I am sure you are thinking of children on the spectrum who tantrum in response to even the smallest change, ADHD children who lose control due to overexcitement, traumatized/anxious children who can become immobilized, or behaviorally challenged children who refuse to go with the flow.

Although it has been continuously recommended you read over the previous section of the chapter as we approach essentials and modifications for other settings, for this topic think: *keep it simple, pare back, slow down*. If the basic structure and rhythm of the lessons is still in its infancy for your individual or small group, keep that as a goal first, so you will have that foundation needed for more explicit instruction in transitions. Then as you slowly, over time, teach the concepts and skills, it will be reassuring for the children to approach transitions as a "time of the day" needing skill practice and will give you a greater vocabulary for preparing them.

Recommended Essentials

Steady not windy
Carefulness with the body
Being like clay, having clear thoughts for flexibility
Managing emotion

Although the three transition time skills—steady, careful, focused— are important, the first two recommended essentials here help address a fundamental lagging skill for dysregulated children: the inability to maintain safe self-control, particularly when going from one thing to another while surrounded by others going from one thing to another. It continues to astound me how many hours of instruction and practice in self-awareness, body awareness, and finding satisfaction in control some children need. Because such children require constant reminders, they can come to believe it is impossible to develop safe self-control. As mentioned in the previous section, the language and teaching "steady, not windy" communicates the skill lag more kindly and instills the hope that no matter how windy you might be, you can become steadier, then steady—even for a moment as you learn. This then allows you to explicitly teach carefulness: starting with steadiness, then moving the body alertly as to avoid hurting yourself, other people, or things.

The next two essentials highlight a fundamental reality transition times create for certain children: They dislike change, have a consequential negative mindset regarding change, and have trouble managing the emotions arising about change. This may be organic for some, or for others an indication of ingrained habits of inflexibility that make so many things so very difficult, leading to discouragement. The feel, look, and imagery of clay can offer another kinder, less judgmental teaching tool for the possibility of skill-building in flexibility. This, combined with the instruction in clear thoughts, can then create a calmer pathway to help the child understand, then manage the emotions that arise in transition times.

Modifying Class Elements

Begin. Besides all the comforting routines and structure you have now established to begin in your setting, you want to ensure the stability of calm throughout the lesson to balance any potential anxiety or habitual patterns of distress regarding transitions. Use the chime practice and any calm breaths that have been established to settle the individual or group. Teach the Transition Time song line by line, perhaps asking the children to do the mountain, then the cloud, then the perching eagle as you sing/recite. If they can conceptually grasp what a transition is, move on to the instruction about what it means to be windy, with a word of caution: An exceptionally concrete child may not have the ability to consider this a metaphor. If so, fall back on "steady/unsteady." Then proceed to the first transition toward centering in your setting. Name every transition in this lesson and offer praise for steadiness, care, and focus.

Centering. The "M and M" breath can be popular with special populations, with the following specialized instructions:

The basic M and M breath: Sit up straight. Place hand on chest, take a deep breath in, close mouth, and make the "m" sound quietly as you exhale. Repeat; then ask, "Can you feel the sound making you calm?"

Special consideration: This breath can give children who enjoy noise making a channel for sound, but can also show up later in unwanted places. Use the breathing ball and be very clear we use it as a breath, with the breath: The sound starts when the ball is as big as it can be, then ends when the ball is as small as it can be.

Warm-up. The warm-up Blast Off may be too much movement for an overly excitable child. Consider using Boat, but point out all the changes your body makes throughout and mention that when we move back and forth, that is the practice of flexibility.

Poses. The eagle flow can be very special for a child who has motor struggles, offering the possibility of feeling finesse in movement. If you want to prioritize a few, start with perching eagle to encourage the feeling of stability, then soaring eagle to offer beauty and easy in movement.

Game. If the complexity of the full Switcheroo game is too much, consider simply teaching the concept of flexibility with the clay and clear thoughts with the jar, as discussed previously. A simple variation on the game might be just saying the word "switcheroo" and asking a child to move to a different spot calmly. Pour on the praise for willingness to change and for being "like clay."

Rest. For children who need soothing simplicity, consider returning to the beautiful garden—something very familiar at this point in our series of lessons. Emphasize that now there are no changes, and our quiet, steady place is always there to help us during times of change.

Centering/Close. As they sit up at the close of the rest time, have them pause and take only calm breaths, and fully prepare them for the transition(s) ahead. Cue them to use whatever skills you were able to teach. Note every part of the transition that is completed, emphasizing how much easier it is when everyone is steady, careful, focused, or flexible like clay.

Teaching and Using Transition Time at Home

Recommended Essentials

Scaffolding transitions to teach independence
Focus on the most important things: for you and your child
Managing emotion for clear thinking and flexibility

Helping your child develop the skills they need to navigate transition times smoothly is perhaps the greatest investment in resiliency you can ever make as a parent. Every transition through life, welcome or unwelcome, offers opportunities and dangers. Young people who know what a transition is, what skills are required, and how to use them can better find the opportunities and minimize the dangers, protecting their physical and mental well-being.

Developing transition time skills at home requires a great deal of scaffolding in early childhood, which can then be gradually and appropriately relinquished by young adulthood. Start with steady: You can expect your child to learn to slow down, become a mountain and attend to the needs of a transition time even at a young age. This develops the expectation that they can practice this skill later in a crowded gymnasium after a game, at the family gathering when it is time to leave, and daily as bedtime approaches. Care is similar: In the inevitable chaos of transitions, it is easy to cast aside attention to details such as collecting your things, remembering your school folder, saying goodbye meaningfully. If you model such care in the early years, it will become a positive habit your child can practice no matter what happens, where they are, or with whom. By late adolescence over years of practice they can then handle the emotion and requirements of launching into adulthood with this steadiness and care.

Transition times offer us a plethora of distractions at home: the riveting toy rather than picking up, that last drink before bedtime, that one last thing you need for the trip. Once you have established and taught, "This is a transition time, we are going from _____ to _____, I need you to help by being steady," you can help yourself and your family with the focus on the "most important thing," or focused prioritization while in transition. This is best taught in the early years by consistency with routines and your ability to focus on what matters, then in later childhood by partnering with your child to decide what is important and when. The fruits of such practice are young adults who can hold a job or meet the requirements for graduation, and adults who can better problem solve in a crisis.

Transition times at home are frequently fraught with emotion because a child is ideally in a safe environment with people who care, and so many changes demanded of the child are not of their own choosing. Your gift is your calm, clear thoughts that teach the foundation of flexibility. A tantrum when it is time to leave a friend's house? Offer understanding for the difficulty of the transition and its emotions, with the calm confidence that we can say "Oh well, we will come back another day;" then recognize flexibility when it is practiced. Didn't pass the driving test? That's hard, but let's see how more practice might help next time. These seemingly small transitions over time offer the development of a useful muscle that will ensure your child will handle the more challenging joys and disappointments of life with positivity and perspective.

Chapter SEVEN
Social Time

Social time, the third time of the day for consideration, asks us to turn our attention to the times we spend nurturing our relationships: our friendships, our families, and all the people who serve us. The Social Times concepts and skills have grown from a need to reclaim some fundamental social understandings and skills that make a civil society work and flourish. The instruction helps clarify for children what people generally do during social times (eat, talk, play—not an exclusive list) and expected and appropriate words and actions that help build relationships, rather than break them (safe, kind). In my experience, this teaching cannot be taken for granted and should be taught to our children continually. As with the instruction on respect, the clarification and skill-building offers already skilled children validation that civility matters, and offers less-skilled children exposure to ideas and skills they may not know from experience.

Social time is appropriately placed here, as the last concept area and skill set, as a kind of culmination of all the other concepts that help children more successfully utilize their social skills in any setting and in any relationship. Respect has been established as an essential foundation for healthy relationships with peers and adults. Calm has offered the quiet steadiness that makes others feel safe and aids in problem solving, Alert has encouraged attentiveness and readiness for all encounters. Learning Time skills have developed positive partnerships with the people who teach us or work with us on a task. Transition Time helped encourage personal responsibility for steadiness and focus during times of change. Hence the Social Time concepts and skills echo and build on previous learning in *Calm and Alert* while offering specifics for this time of the day.

Many children have a gravitational pull toward eating, talking freely, and playing at any time, so the instruction that there are different times with other expectations was designed to support clarification. In a school setting after age five, social times generally are snack and lunch times, and indoor and outdoor play times such as recess. Family gatherings, play dates, restaurant visits, community gatherings, and sports events can also be social times. Although there can be overlap with the other times taught (e.g., learning can happen during social times, and transitions are always some part of social times), the hope is to set social times apart so children do not make inadvertent mistakes like socializing in math, goofing around while playing in a soccer game, or insisting on eating when everyone is packing up to go somewhere. It has offered adults vocabulary to steer children toward appropriate behavior ("Be careful to be safe and kind") and avoid inappropriate behavior ("This is not a social time right now").

The instruction in this chapter offers more explicit teaching about the six basic feelings (happy, sad, angry, scared, surprised, disgusted) and their importance at social times. This includes: Everyone has feelings that need to be respected; people's faces can give us clues about how they feel; it is beneficial to say and do things that are kind and encourage happiness for ourselves and others; it is beneficial to avoid doing things that are unsafe because it effects our relationships; we can become calm and work out problems if our feelings get strong. This establishes an instructional pathway for the development of empathy and connectedness with real people in real time, some of the beautiful fruits of mindfulness practices so needed in our world today.

Social Time Concepts

Social time:
A time for connections with friends and family
when we are eating, talking freely, or playing

Skills needed = safe and kind

Teaching Social Time as a Class

Begin
Centering
Warm-up
Poses
Game
Rest
Centering/Close

If you have been teaching the lessons as a series, this could be the final lesson and cause for celebration for all we have accomplished and learned. All of the *Calm and Alert* skills are social skills that help us in our relationships with friends, adult helpers/teachers, and family. The warm-up simulates eating with others and sharing happily, and the game is highly interactive to allow the children to practice skills and notice how safety and kindness make everyone happy and connections enjoyable.

Lesson 7: Social Time

Begin. Begin today by saying that our lesson is a celebration of all our learning in *Calm and Alert* class, with a focus on our third time of the day, Social Time: a time for friends (and other people). All of our skills help us connect with other people and make and keep friends. Continue with other routine reminders about the flow of the class and all that usually happens.

Have the children place a hand over their heart, and tell them that our hearts keep us alive each day by beating. Have them make a soft fist and simulate the beating of the heart by gently pulsing the fist over the area of the heart and saying "lub dub, lub dub, lub dub" as they do so. Then teach that the heart is the center of all our caring for our friends and other people. Respect and caring start here.

Consider this variation on the chime practice that draws attention to the heart:

Chime Practice: Heart Focus

Keep your hand over your heart
Ring chime, as you listen,
feel your heart beating
Lead children in 3–5 slow, deep breaths;
as you breathe, bring kindness and
softness into your heart
Ring chime, as you listen,
feel your heart beating

End by saying, "Let's see if we can keep our hearts soft, kind, and open today in our practice." Then teach the Social Time song line by line, pausing to teach things such as: "When is a time we eat or talk or play together?" (in your setting). Highlight the importance of safety and kindness at all times with all people.

Social Time Song

It is social time
It is social time
Time for friends (& family)
Time for friends (& family)
Eating, talking, playing
Safe and kind
Social time
Social time

Continue to offer scaffolding for the transitions to preparing the room for practice, reminding them of our learning from last time about transitions, and praising all the established practices that you hopefully see at this point in the lesson series!

Centering. When the group is settled, with everyone seated cross-legged, straight and tall, teach them the heart breaths—both calm and alert versions. Mention that sometimes you might need to become calm with your friends; other times, you may need to become more alert.

Heart breath: Sit up straight, place hands on top of head with curved fingers. Take a deep breath in and bring hands up in a curving motion like the top of a heart shape; breathe out and arch hands as they come down into the point of the heart. This can also be done as an alert breath with the same movements, but a quick breath in and out.

Have your feeling pictures and paint chip ready for instruction. Hold up the group of six feelings and say, "These are feelings, the six feelings everyone has at different times. Let's name them." Hold each up and have the group name them (with an older group, give them the challenge of doing it as quickly as possible, or name as many words as they know describing the feeling). Then say, "Feelings are important when we are with friends and other people. They can help us know when things are safe and kind." Then hold up the happy face and draw their attention to the eyes, the smile, or any other indicators or clues that this person is happy, teaching that people's faces can help us know how they are feeling. Hold up the other feeling faces and do the same. Hold up the paint chip and remind the children that we previously learned feelings can be strong (point to red) or calm (point to pink), and we can use our calm breaths to help our feelings stay in the calm zone and solve problems with friends. Other instructional points about feelings you can highlight include:

Instructional Points About Feelings

- When we are safe and kind, people usually like it. Offering safety and kindness makes us happy, and also makes other people happy when they see and receive these from us.

- When we are unsafe or unkind, people usually do not like it. We might notice it makes them sad, mad, scared, or disgusted. We can notice their faces, and help solve a problem or change our words and actions to avoid this.

- People remember what we do and say. If we are safe and kind, they remember feeling happy when they are with us and will want to spend more time with us or be our friend. When we are unsafe or unkind, they also remember, and then may be cautious about being our friends. Practicing safety and kindness helps all our relationships be better.

- When our feelings get into the strong zone (hold up paint chip and point to dark red) with friends, we might make unsafe or unkind mistakes. We should take a calm breath to help us get back into the calm zone.

Today we will be practicing kindness and safety in all our movements and activities, and noticing people's faces and how they feel.

Warm-up. Introduce this warm-up by saying, "Now we are going to make some cookies to share with our friends!"

Making Cookies

Sit up straight and tall on your mat with your legs out in front of you. Open your legs out so they form a "V."

Pretend there is a bowl between your legs and we are ready to make cookies for our friends. Reach up with your right hand and grab an ingredient (flour) and put it in the bowl. Reach up with your left hand and grab another ingredient (oatmeal). Reach behind for butter on one side, then reach behind on the other for honey, eggs, raisins (or other ingredients of your choosing) and place them in the bowl. Pretend to mix the dough by making a big circle with your hands one way, then the other. Put out one forearm and imagine this is our cookie sheet. With the other hand, pretend to scoop dough up and onto the sheet.

To bake, pretend to open the oven and place the cookies in. While you are waiting for them to bake, sing/recite a *Calm and Alert* song. After the song is finished, ask, "What are some kind words we might use as we share our cookies?" hoping for answers such as "please," "thank you," "would you like some?" etc. When they are done, say "Ding" and take out the cookies. Take a big breath in and blow on them to cool. Then share your cookies with a friend. Smile.

Bring the warm-up to a close with the chime sound. Have the children put their hands on their bellies, take a deep breath, brush the crumbs off their hands, and say, "Aren't we lucky to have food and friends?" Hold up the happy face and say, "I saw lots of people looking happy!"

Poses. By this point regulation may be established enough that you can say, "When I count to three, stand like a mountain in the middle of your mat," and the transition to standing may be smooth and quick. Once standing, tell the children that when we are safe and kind we are like beautiful stars shining our lights on the world and making it a better place. Then teach the star breath and the star, noticing safety and steadiness throughout.

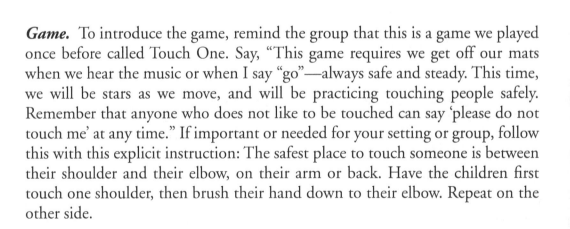

Stars

Star breath: Lace fingers in front of chest. Take a quick breath in and bring laced hands up to ceiling; exhale, and release hands out to sides and down while wiggling fingers (twinkling).

Star: Starting in mountain, place hands on hips and hop legs out to a "V," keeping stance steady and feet on mat. Pause and feel steadiness. Now bring hands out to a "T" position. "Twinkle" by wiggling fingers, circling wrists, or making fists then quickly shooting fingers outward. *Variation:* hands overhead, bend forward and touch ground; keep one hand on the ground and lift the second hand up for a twist, repeat on other side.

Game. To introduce the game, remind the group that this is a game we played once before called Touch One. Say, "This game requires we get off our mats when we hear the music or when I say "go"—always safe and steady. This time, we will be stars as we move, and will be practicing touching people safely. Remember that anyone who does not like to be touched can say 'please do not touch me' at any time." If important or needed for your setting or group, follow this with this explicit instruction: The safest place to touch someone is between their shoulder and their elbow, on their arm or back. Have the children first touch one shoulder, then brush their hand down to their elbow. Repeat on the other side.

Touch One: Star Variation

Have child/children stand like a mountain in the middle of the mat or space. Put on lively music and give instruction to move either like a skipping or galloping star, by keeping their arms near their sides and twinkling their hands while they move. When the music stops, children stop. You then say: "Touch one elbow to someone else's elbow." Say, "If you feel safe and respected, smile at the person you are touching." If this goes well, repeat and have them touch shoulders, which is usually funnier. Praise them for inviting people to touch, solving problems, and other kindnesses. Point out how much fun the game is when everyone is safe.

Bring the group back to their mats, standing like mountain, with a calm breath. Then have them raise their arms, find their rain, and become a puddle for a few breaths before transitioning to rest time.

Rest. For this rest time I am offering the Night Sky as imagery, but if your group has had multiple lessons already, also consider allowing them to pick their favorite beautiful place. If you do so, simply get the story started (sky, field, stream) and then say, "Where is your favorite place to picture?"

Rest Time Script: The Night Sky

"Lay on your back, belly, or side comfortably and become still on your mat by using your deep, calm breaths. Notice your feet, legs, torso, arms, hands, neck, and head and become still. This is how we rest our bodies.

Now we will rest our minds and heart with a story:

Picture a beautiful blue sky and the sun shining down on you. Imagine a big field and see yourself walk, skip, run, or hop through the field. You hear, then see, a steady stream and walk beside it. The bubbling sounds seem to say 'lay all your cares in my waters' and you take any cares you have and imagine them washed away by the stream. You keep walking until you reach a gate and look up at the sky. As you watch, the sun begins to set and the sky becomes darker and darker until you see the night sky full of stars.

Imagine becoming a star yourself and shooting up to twinkle in the beautiful sky, surrounded by stars everywhere to keep you company. Can you see the full moon also shining with you? Rest here. Notice your quiet, steady place as you twinkle, knowing it is always with you."

Pause here and allow silence for a few minutes.

"Now it is time to say goodbye to this beautiful place, but we never have to leave our quiet, steady place—it is always with you. Shoot out of the sky, and as you land become a person again. Walk back through the field to _____ (their present setting). Turn on your side and pause there. Bring your knees into your chest, wrap your arms around your knees and give yourself a hug. Now push yourself up to sitting."

If you anticipate this being your final lesson, be sure to emphasize that all the beautiful places we have visited are inside them and that they always have their quiet, steady place to help them whenever they need it.

Centering/Close. As you see the group come to sitting, praise them for our beautiful practice together today. Ask them to notice how they feel and decide if a calm or alert breath might help them. Then lead the group in a few heart breaths, letting each individual decide whether to do it as an alert or a calm breath.

Also praise them for how well they have learned to smoothly roll up their mats, self-check for steadiness before they go to the mat bin, and neatly place the mats in the bin. When the mat bin is tidy, it is a flower of respect for everyone.

End with either the Social Time song, or if this is your last lesson, the *Calm and Alert* song learned at the beginning of the journey!

Calm and Alert Song

I am calm
I am calm
And alert
And alert
Every day at home
And every day at school
Calm, alert
Calm, alert

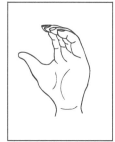
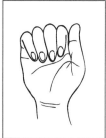

Calm and Alert Lesson: Social Time

Lesson 7

Grade/Group_____   Date_____

Materials needed:
Pictures of six feelings
Paint chip with gradations of color: red/pink preferred

Lesson

Begin:
Social Time song
Instruction about six feelings

Centering:
Heart breath: calm and alert, with instruction about being both

Warm-up:
Making Cookies

Poses:
Star breath
Star

Game:
Touch One: shoulder to elbow touching, with instruction about safe touching

Rest:
The Night Sky (or a place of beauty of your choosing)

Centering/Close:
Social Time or *Calm and Alert* song

Teaching and Using Social Time in Other Settings

Recommended Essentials

Learning to connect with other people
Understanding feelings and how they affect relationships
Personal space and touching other people
Explicit safety and kindness

For many children with lagging social skills due to cognitive or developmental delays, autism, impulsivity and attentional issues, anxiety, behavioral challenges, or shy temperaments, social times can be their most longed for and most confusing times of a day. The Social Time instruction offers practice in body awareness, safety and kindness, self-awareness, personal space, and managing and noticing feelings, which can lay a foundation of hope for connecting with other people.

Spending extra time teaching the second essential—understanding feelings and how they affect relationships—is a worthy endeavor. Each of the six feelings and the teaching points highlighted in the previous section on centering can be rich material for many months of practice, review, and in-the-moment feedback. Fostering the development of self-awareness in managing feelings with the calm breaths and clear thoughts to stay in the calm zone can also have a positive impact on forming friendships. So many misunderstandings and problems stem from this essential skill area!

The other essentials (personal space, touching, safety and kindness) are easily practiced through modifications to the lesson and repetition. The mats form a concrete boundary for feedback about where your body is in space and moving safely. The warm-ups and games (Making Cookies, Touch One, and others), which require safe touching and movement around other people, offer opportunities for explicit feedback in these areas. Concrete instruction about kind words and actions and noticing the happiness felt when a child successfully connects with friends have also been effective. It has been the greatest pleasure to see the natural inclusivity of this lesson, with or without modifications.

Modifying Class Elements

Begin. Hopefully by this lesson you can feel the benefits of all you have done to establish consistent ways of starting the practice in your setting: the children anticipating the chime practice and song, and your ability to draw on past learning in other lessons. The elements of "begin" in the class lesson should serve any population, with the additional awareness of the heart unless your population is too literal. Consider using the Social Time song for additional line-by-line instruction, based on the needs of your individual or group. Spend time, for example, naming times we eat, what we eat and how we eat, noting appropriate voice level when we talk, or various kinds of play appropriately done with friends. With certain special populations, the Social Time song used instructionally could span many months or could be used daily before a social time.

Centering. If you have not used mats or some other floor aid with a boundary for practice, consider using something for this lesson. I have found the mats to be the best tool for instruction in body awareness and personal space, and the affect it has on other people (see the Respect chapter for instruction about mats). You can ask, "Are you in your space?" and allow the child to look themselves over and adjust their body. You can use the mats to point out how safe it feels when everyone has a space they "stay" in, and then when/if you play a game, the mats are a reference point.

Use of the heart breath, as well as the feeling pictures and teaching points as suggested previously, are recommended. If lagging social skills is a concern for your population, consider spreading the instruction out over a number of lessons.

Warm-up. Many variations on Making Cookies can maintain the same teaching hopes, such as the happiness of sharing, kind words that matter to people, fun. You could make a pizza or a sandwich or some other favorite food with similar movements. You can also return to previous instruction about being "serious, not too silly" with food around friends.

Poses. The star pose does require more balance and steadiness than the mountain pose, so spend extra time going back and forth between mountain and star if needed. Twinkling is fun but stimulating! Always return to the mountain or puddle if things get windy.

Game. If possible, play some variation of Touch One with the instruction about appropriate touch—of course gauging the capability of your population. For some, it may be best to start with touching a place on their own body when you say "touch one," if their body awareness is minimal. You may also want to spend extra time talking about touching as one way of connecting with people, but it has to be safe and at appropriate times. You can bring back the feeling pictures here to aid instruction in how safe touch feels. There are many special needs children who need constant instruction in this area of self-regulation: when to touch, when not to touch, gentleness, asking permission to touch and respecting the answer, avoiding hurtfulness. The reward for the extra, explicit instruction is the possibility of being included in games with typically developing peers.

Rest. Use your discretion about what image would best serve your individual or group, but in keeping with the theme, add something about the happiness of connecting with people. For example, if you visit the garden, mention friends being there, or sitting in the cozy house with family. Use the words kind and safe, and draw their attention to their quiet, steady place inside, as always.

Centering/Close. Bring your child or group back to sitting, celebrating the happy feeling we had today as we connected with our friends. Finish with the heart breaths and even placing their hands on the hearts once more, and the song. Then lead the group in any way that is now routine for closing your practice together.

Teaching and Using Social Time at Home

Recommended Essentials

All the basics start at home: feelings, kindness, safety
Helping your child understand social times
with family, friends, and in the community

Of the three times of the day discussed, social time is probably the most comfortably familiar for you as a parent because so many times at home with family and friends are social times. I want to validate and congratulate you for the tireless work you do daily, in real time with real people, to help your child be astute about feelings, kindness and safety. No matter what your home circumstances might be, those thousands of smiles, sympathetic nods, hugs during tears, hours of listening, small and large kindnesses, discipline, and respectful treatment of your child all contribute to forming a well-socialized human being. It is one of the essential privileges of parenting that we can have this kind of formative effect on the development of the little people given to us. The more socialization you can do in your home, in the safety of your love, the stronger your child's foundation will be in all their relationships.

The only other essential this third time of day could offer you in parenting is demarcating the difference between social times at home with family and friends from social times in more public places such as restaurants, schools, churches, playing fields, social media, etc. There should be a higher degree of self-awareness and self-control expected during more public social times, which is sometimes confusing for children. The vocabulary could offer you the opportunity to talk about expectations in various places regarding how feelings are expressed, being polite as a kindness, and what safe words and actions look like outside of your home.

Chapter EIGHT
The Fruits of Practice

"The fruits of practice" is a lovely phrase that refers to benefits a practitioner may notice in their body, mind, or spirit that they may attribute to their work with the practices. This chapter turns its attention to the fruits of the practices taught through *Calm and Alert*: both internal fruits the children have shown or shared, and external fruits the adults that serve them have observed or noted in various ways. I hope to shed light on the benefits of this practice that will satisfy those interested in measuring effects through assessments and data, and those interested in seeing the effects through personal accounts. To do so, this chapter offers an exclusive structure.

The chapter is organized using a very simplified version of a framework that has helped many public schools discuss how to think about and teach all their children, depending on their skill level and how they respond to instruction. It begins with a triangle divided into three tiers:

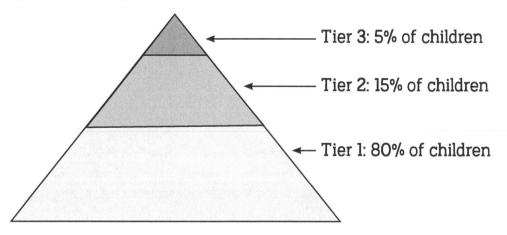

The basic headings of the chapter are organized by tier, and the subsections allow the readers interested in measurement tools and quantitative data to find satisfaction in "measuring the fruits" and those interested in effects shown through personal accounts to find satisfaction in "seeing the fruits." Reading both is an interesting study in the meaning of effectiveness and the measuring of effectiveness in this nascent field. Here is what to expect:

> **The Fruits of *Calm and Alert* in Tier 1**
> > Overview
> > Measuring the Fruits in Tier 1
> > Seeing the Fruits in Tier 1
>
> **The Fruits of *Calm and Alert* in Tier 2**
> > Overview
> > Measuring the Fruits in Tier 2
> > Seeing the Fruits in Tier 2
>
> **The Fruits of *Calm and Alert* in Tier 3**
> > Overview
> > Seeing the Fruits in Tier 3

Tier 1 describes most children (usually about 80%) who respond well to and easily learn from the basic curriculums and teaching approaches offered. All the lessons in the first section of each chapter were designed to start in **Tier 1**. If you are a yoga instructor or parent reader, this tier includes the children who respond easily to your general teaching style or parenting approach.

Tier 2 describes some children (usually about 15%) who do not as easily learn from the approaches offered in **Tier 1** and need a more explicit, targeted approach to skill building, with the hope that more explicit instruction will help the children "return" to **Tier 1**. The recommended essentials and modifications offered in the second section of each chapter were developed with this group in mind. If you are a therapist or special educator, many of the children you serve are part of **Tier 2**. If you are a yoga teacher or parent, these are the children you have to be innovative with, asking: "What can I do differently to reach this child?"

Tier 3 describes the smallest group of children (usually about 5%) who do not easily learn from approaches in **Tier 1 or 2**, often have some type of known disability, and need very specialized, individualized instruction for long periods of their development. The modifications in the second section of each chapter can address some **Tier 3** needs, but an individualized plan for *Calm and Alert* reflective of the child's unique profile would be indicated in this tier. Many therapists serve this tier intensely (special educators primarily), and parents rely on a supportive professional team to help them raise and educate their **Tier 3** child.

The Fruits of Calm and Alert in Tier 1

Overview

The primary goal of the *Calm and Alert* class for Tier 1 is to teach the six unit areas to all students ages five to seven in kindergarten through second grade, to enhance and strengthen self-regulation and social skill development by age seven. For children ages eight to 10 in grades three to five, the skills are reviewed and practiced for maintaining skill mastery. A secondary goal has been to develop a method of skill acquisition that would be easily generalizable for children, teachers, and parents in multiple settings at school and home.

I have implemented the program in the following way to reach these goals:

> Kindergarten: 18 lessons (3 for each unit area) throughout school year
> Grade 1: 6 lessons each fall (1 from each unit area); others as needed
> Grade 2: 6 lessons each fall (1 from each unit area); others as needed
> Grade 3: 4 lessons for review of skills in fall, called "applied *Calm and Alert*"
> Grades 4–5: 4 lessons in fall related to self-management, building on the *Calm and Alert* foundation

Measuring the Fruits in Tier 1

Original research. The first formal year of the *Calm and Alert* class (2009) I conducted an action research study, a common tool in education, using survey and personal account data from teachers and parents in the grade level group involved in the pilot year. In the surveys, I asked questions concerning the skills I was teaching in the class and whether there was observable evidence of mastery in various school settings and at home. I was most interested in discerning whether the skills were being used by students throughout the school day in classrooms, the cafeteria, playground, and other classes such as music and art, at home and extra-curricular activities. Results were promising. The group as a whole showed improvement in self-regulation at various times of the school day and individual students exhibited skill mastery and generalization in a number of instruction areas (McGlauflin, 2010).

Since that time, I have also sought research partners at local universities, and in 2015 a social work intern from the University of New England conducted a case study of the *Calm and Alert* program by conducting interviews with 12 teachers on the efficacy, challenges, and overall perception of the class. The results were generally very positive, with teachers reporting enthusiasm for the class' effectiveness in "helping them teach" by explicit instruction in self-regulation and social skills. There were many supportive comments about my approach as a practitioner, the comfortable way the practices have been brought to the school, the effects on the school culture, and the power of asking children to look within for skill development (Perkins, 2015).

Assessment tools. I am an advocate for collecting data to inform effective teaching and skill acquisition, and offer two assessment tools in Appendix 1 with that goal in mind. However, currently in my public school setting there is at once a pressured expectation to assess, and an unhealthy exhaustion for educators and children asked to meet that demand. When there has been a healthy balance between expectation and available energy, I have used the following tools for Tier 1:

Calm and Alert Teacher Rating Scale. For use in Tier 1, this scale can be filled out by a classroom teacher or the "calm and alert" teacher on every student in the general class. At minimum, rate students before the classes/skills are taught (pre) and after the classes/skills have finished being taught (post). You can also score it midway through the sessions to help inform your teaching. This data can be used to measure the effectiveness of the class, or afterwards to inform which children need further intervention in determined areas. The 12 items explicitly name the skills taught.

Calm and Alert Student Self-Assessment. This scale is most appropriate for children ages seven and older to fill out on their own, but could be used with six-year-olds with adult support. The items highlight the most critical skills taught through the class, and can give an adult valuable information about a child's self-awareness regarding their skills, understanding, and behavior. This measure can be given before an adult teaches the skills, at a midway point, and post class or intervention. I have used it primarily at the end of my Grade 2 lessons, after most children have had the class for three years.

Seeing the Fruits in Tier 1

The School Culture

The lobby fills each morning with 50 or more children waiting to go down to their classes. The energy mounts as the time draws near, with more children talking, the noise volume increasing, small bodies moving. An adult with a chime rings it once, and as the sound is received, children quiet. The adult says, "Take a calm breath," and the group does so. The adult then says, "Be steady like a mountain," and most children stand tall and still. This allows the adult to more easily direct children calmly to class.

Debbie, the cafeteria teacher, overseas sometimes 120 noisy, wiggly children in the lunch room multiple periods a day, and uses the practice of the chime sound and deep breaths periodically to bring some calm to the setting. The setting is anything but ideal and only half of the students, at best, are attentively practicing. But the few that are practicing are earnest and serious, their bodies visibly moving up and down with the inhale and exhale. Their small calmness offers to bring the noise and sometimes pandemonium down just a notch so that someone can finish a sandwich in peace.

"Calm and Alert has created a culture of calm at our school," shared a first-grade teacher.

The Classroom

A third-grade teacher has established "chime helper" each day as one of the many helping jobs in her classroom. On this day, the chime helper, Alex, keeps the chime in his desk. He takes it out as the class gets loud, walks up to the teacher, and says, "I think we need the chime practice now." He then leads the class in listening to the chime, taking the three breaths, and listening once more. He returns to his desk and puts the chime back in for next time.

A kindergarten teacher lines up her class for lunch and says, "Are you steady?" She then sings the Transition Time song as the class walks through the halls.

The Children

Lanky, olive-skinned Janet with shy nervousness asked me after class, "Where did you get your chime?" I told her and asked her why she wanted to know. She replied: "I am asking for a chime for Christmas because my family is crazy and I want to use it when they need it."

Talkative, always looking worried Marly, age six, saw me in the hall and said, "My dad is in the hospital because he had too many muddy thoughts and needed help," which I later learned referred to a psychiatric hospitalization. The concepts of "clear" and "muddy" thoughts helped her understand what was happening for her dad in a non-judgmental way.

The Parents

A mother attending a school assembly at which the chime practice was used said, "I felt a presence."

Another who helps with fundraising asked if a local coffee roaster could name a specialty decaf coffee "Calm and Alert" that could be sold to the community to raise funds for a new playground.

"Are you the one that sings those songs with the hand motions?" asked a parent when we first met. "My son is teaching everyone in our family those songs!"

The Fruits of Calm and Alert in Tier 2

Overview

The *Calm and Alert* concepts and skills can be very useful with **Tier 2** children, particularly for those who exhibit lagging skills in the six concept areas. The goal for use in **Tier 2** is to identify skills that need more instruction after the basic lessons have been taught. A plan is developed to target those needed skills and focus instruction in those areas for six weeks, always hoping skills develop adequately enough that the targeted instruction is no longer needed.

I offer both daily and weekly *Calm and Alert* interventions. For highly dysregulated children in **Tier 2**, I offer a daily morning "check in" for 15 minutes during which the primary goal is to "become steady." The instruction includes learning to sit like a mountain in a chair, listening and breathing through the chime practice, and learning to choose an activity that will help a child become calm such as eating, coloring, reading a story about practicing, or playing with clay. For others needing targeted instruction in **Tier 2**, I offer weekly instruction for 20–30 minutes in small groups in areas of need.

Measuring the Fruits in Tier 2

By late November in the course of a usual school year, most children have had the **Tier 1** *Calm and Alert* instruction in their classrooms, and teachers have filled out the pre- and post-sections of the teacher assessment. True to the tier model, approximately 80%–85% of students K-2 meet the standard in the six unit areas at that time as noted in the post-section of the assessment. Students who receive a "rarely meets" in the post measure are identified for targeted instruction in those areas, often taught in small groups with other children with a similar need. Children who receive "partial meets" are considered for intervention, depending on the area, the frequency the skills are lagging, and whether the classroom teacher feels it can be addressed in the classroom practice.

The Calm and Alert Teacher/Therapist Assessment used previously (Appendix 1) can be used for intervention purposes by selecting appropriate unit areas or particular skills, and scoring them after each session or at the beginning/end of an intervention cycle. The Student Self-Assessment can also be used in this way, primarily as a tool for raising self-awareness. The goal of the intervention cycle is for the child to earn a "meets" in the intervention session, but should also show improvement as reported by the classroom teacher.

I never lose sight of the reality that self-regulation and social skill mastery is dependent on many variables and some children need many years or more of instruction to help them develop this mastery. Pressure to perform, increased demands on immature executive functioning areas of the brain, less outdoor and free playtime, and environmental and organic deficits all contribute to lagging self-regulation. I hope we can all maintain our compassion for the challenges modern children face and the story their behavior tells us.

The Children

Red haired, freckle-faced Scott, age five, who had many challenges controlling his body, hated the class with a passion at the beginning—he could not stay on his mat, complained fiercely every class, and did not follow any directions for weeks and weeks. By the 18th week of the class and multiple intervention cycles, he could stay on his mat more than half the time, could follow half the directions and, best of all, would ask when we were having it again because "now I like it."

Seven-year-old Harry had a chubby, round face with dimples and thick glasses. Being physically larger than his peers made *Calm and Alert* class challenging and he could easily get emotional about small things. Every class he would cry at least once and say, "I can't do it." I would often smile and say, "Oh, but you can. I know how hard it is, let your breath help you." After many weeks, one class he still cried, and loudly took breaths, saying, "I am doing it."

Janel, who daily faces the instability of addiction and domestic violence, said, "I like picturing that quiet, steady stream at home. It makes me feel better."

James, who had been discouraged about his schoolwork for some time, liked the clear thought: "I can do this even if it is hard." His attitude began to improve. When asked how he did it he said, "When the muddy thoughts start coming, I say 'no, no, no' to them and 'yes, yes, yes' to the clear thoughts."

The Teachers

A first-grade teacher in January came to me in tears because, since the holiday break, more than five of the 18 children in her class were "so dysregulated" it was "like a wild fire of muddy thoughts and windiness." It was making instructional control of her class difficult. Together we designed a Tier 2 intervention in which she identified eight children who needed more skill building, targeting clear thoughts and steadiness. Once per week the identified children stayed with me for a *Calm and Alert* class, while the teacher took the remainder of the students to another location to work on literacy skills. The targeted group slowly improved each week and by week four, children who consistently were steady and clear for two classes or more could join the literacy group. The teacher was cheered. By week five the targeted group was only three children, a small enough number that we did a *Calm and Alert* class with the whole group again on week six. The teacher's instructional control was restored with the majority of students steady and clear, who could now be role models for the remaining Tier 2 children.

The Parents

One mom reported: "I was angry one day at home and my daughter said, 'You need to talk a calm breath right now mom.'"

A parent asked for an appointment because her son was "completely out of control" at home—tantrums over the smallest problem, regularly yelling at family members explosively. I taught her the calm breaths, the mountain and the puddle, and sent her home with handouts. Within a month, with cueing, her son could become calm when upset and would spontaneously use the puddle when he started becoming upset.

The Fruits of Calm and Alert in Tier 3

Overview

When I first began my journey bringing the *Calm and Alert* practices to the school I serve, the teachers and I hoped it would especially benefit those students in **Tier 3** with a high degree of behavioral dysregulation, who adults would say "need it most." I have been regularly humbled and have learned the most about the practices from these remarkable children. What they have taught me is how very difficult and sometimes painful the practices are for them. If your senses are hyper aroused, the sound of the chime can feel like fingernails on a blackboard. If you have a trauma history, closing your eyes may mean the arrival of an upsetting memory. If you are on the autistic spectrum, a speck of dirt on your mat can completely consume you. If your body feels out of control, being steady like a mountain could not be more foreign. Approaching children in **Tier 3** with the practices should be done with the greatest gentleness, the greatest compassion, and the greatest respect.

My experience in using *Calm and Alert* with the **Tier 3** population has been limited to times when I am given a special invitation to serve a **Tier 3** student, a self-contained special education classroom, or a **Tier 3** student is included in my class or in whole school activities. Hence, my sample size is small and my stories few. I start by learning all I can from teachers about their individual needs, and start cautiously with the basics, slowly proceed when the child is ready, and reteach often. In my experience, the practices (when they can be used) are only one small piece of a very complex array of services, but they can bring moments of hope and joy to the tier who may "need it most."

The Children

Feisty Lisa came to school every day discombobulated: backpack askew, things falling out of her bag, yelling greetings to everyone, pushing peers. This dysregulation continued the entire day, with unsafe, out-of-control behavior needing multiple time-outs and behavior calls requiring removal from her classroom. I offered to begin her day "becoming steady" in my office for

---

the first 15 minutes before going to her class. She was asked to sit down in a chair at a table, take deep breaths, and either eat a snack, color, or play with a piece of putty for 10 minutes. For many months, she needed repeated instruction on "becoming steady." One day she was finally sitting steady in her chair after she arrived independently. She quietly said, "Did you notice how steady I was?" Simultaneously, Lisa was taught to do the puddle pose rather than sit and take a break when out of control, and the number of breaks needed diminished in this time.

I was invited to teach a very short, 15-minute weekly class to a self-contained classroom serving six children ages five to nine on the autistic spectrum, with lagging skills in language and mobility. We did the chime practice, sang the *Calm and Alert* song and practiced being a mountain. In two sessions they were quiet enough to listen to the chime and could take at least one calm breath. In four weeks they could sit like a mountain, sing parts of the songs, take calm breaths, and even become calm if upset using the practices during the short class. After six sessions, one eight-year-old girl would say "I am calm" when she was sitting quietly.

Blue-eyed, dark-haired, seven-year-old Billy stood at a whole school assembly and led the student body in the chime practice. Although usually severely behaviorally challenged, on this day with perfect control he said into a microphone, "Sit up straight" and then struck the chime. All 340 students were still as the sound lingered. He then led the assembly by saying, "Take a deep breath in," waited, then, "Take a second deep breath in," then, "Take a third breath in," and the community visibly calmed. Next he struck the chime again and all listened. The practice allowed Billy to be a role model, help the entire school body practice together, and feel successfully steady for a few minutes. The respect for Billy and for the practice was palpable.

Centering

As this book ends, I hope you will pause, take a deep breath, and reflect on your intention for reading this book. An intention is a soft beacon of yearning leading you toward something you want for yourself, others, or the world. My intention for writing this book was to offer you a practical and inspiring guide for bringing body, mind, and breath practices to the teaching of self-regulation and social skills for children. I hope my intention has matched at least one of your beacons, and that our lights together will draw us optimistically toward the future through the children we touch.

Thank you for reading this book. Your interest in and willingness to devote time to reading about this topic places you with millions of other people around the globe who consider and practice mindfulness and yoga, hoping to live optimally and to serve our new generations with the practices. The world's children need all of us right now with urgency. Never forget that watering respect in your heart, taking one calm breath, being alert to the world and people around you, and holding all the times of our daily lives dear is worthy work that matters.

> *May all children and the adults that serve them be healthy.*
> *May all children and the adults that serve them be happy.*
> *May all children and the adults that serve them*
> *be free to teach, learn and live optimally.*

Appendix 1

Calm and Alert Assessment Tools

For your convenience scripts, lesson plans, assessment tools and graphics may be downloaded at pesi.com/calmandalert

· Calm and Alert Teacher/Therapist Assessment ·

Name_____

(M) Shows skill most of the time
(P): Shows skill part of the time
(R): Shows skill rarely

Respect	Pre	Mid	Post
1. Exhibits caring, gentleness, and seriousness toward self and others.			
2. Exhibits caring, gentleness, and seriousness toward environment and materials.			

Calm			
3. Is physically and emotionally steady while still or moving.			
4. Uses strategies such as feeling words, breath poses to soothe self.			

Alert			
5. Appears rested and awake.			
6. Is ready to learn: body steady and quiet, eyes on speaker, performs required tasks willingly.			

Learning Time			
7. Is able to listen, focus, and follow directions during learning times.			
8. Can name clear and muddy thoughts about learning and is able to practice having clear thoughts about learning.			

Transition Time			
9. Is steady, careful, and focused during transitions.			
10. Exhibits flexibility during times of change.			

Social Time			
11. Is safe, kind, and in control during social times.			
12. Can problem solve with peers calmly.			

178

· Calm and Alert Self-Assessment ·

My name_____

	1. Just right	2. I need more practice	3. I need a lot more practice
I am calm	1	2	3
I am alert	1	2	3
I am respectful	1	2	3
I am focused	1	2	3
I listen	1	2	3
I am steady	1	2	3
I follow directions	1	2	3
I do my job	1	2	3
I am safe	1	2	3
I am in control	1	2	3

Appendix 2

Reproducibles

1. Mind, body, breath icons

Body

Mind

Breath

Happy

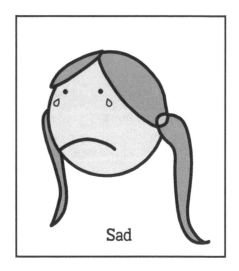

Sad

Scared

Disgusted

Angry

Surprised

Clear Jar

Muddy Jar

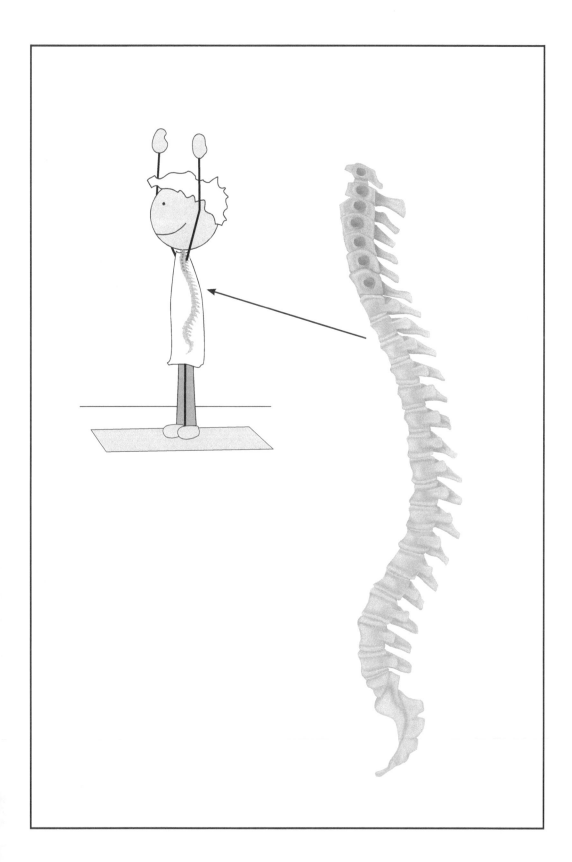

185

Appendix 3

In Support of Calm and Alert: A Literature Review

Calm and Alert was developed to help all children master foundational skills they need for success in the 21st century. It has developed since the turn of the century, when the research on using yoga and mindfulness with children to teach self-regulation and social skills was very new. I offer here a rationale and overview of the research I have followed and used to support this work in its development, drawing from the fields of social/emotional learning, yoga with children, mindfulness with children, and self-regulation.

As supported in the literature, and based on my inquiries and observations, this skill set children most need for overall success is comprehensively, most accurately, and best described as the self-regulation of learning-related social skills (Moffitt et al., 2010; Schunk, 2008; Pelco & Reed-Victor, 2007; Bodrova & Leong, 2005; McCabe, Cunnington & Brooks-Gunn, 2004; McClelland, Morrison & Holmes, 2000). Self-regulation has been defined generally as a "wide variety of capabilities involved in regulating emotion and behavior of the self" (McCabe et al., 2004, p. 342), theoretically as "the process whereby students activate and sustain cognitions and behaviors systematically oriented toward the attainment of their learning goals" (Schunk, 2008, p. 465), and perhaps most thoughtfully as "a deep, internal mechanism that underlies mindful, intentional and thoughtful behaviors of children" (Bodrova & Leong, 2005, p. 55). Those seeking practical language suited to children will most appreciate this definition: "The capacity to control one's impulses, both to stop doing something and to start doing something" (Bodrova & Leong, 2005, p. 55). Self-regulation and self-control are often used interchangeably, although self-regulation appears to be a more comprehensive term for purposes of this work.

The term "learning-related social skills" (LRSS) is appealing because it broadens the traditional definition of social skills by encompassing both interpersonal and work-related skills such as self-regulation, listening, following directions, participating appropriately in groups, organization, responsibility, independence, and the ability to focus and attend (McClelland et al., 2000). The term can also include skills noted in the literature under executive function such as response inhibition, emotional control, sustained attention, task initiation, flexibility, and goal-directed persistence (Dawson & Guare, 2010; Moffitt et al., 2010), considered essential for school and life success.

The importance of such skills on school and life success is well documented in the literature (Committee for Children, 2016; Shanker, 2013; Mind and Life Education Research Network, 2012; Dawson & Guare, 2010; Moffitt et al., 2010; Blair & Diamond, 2008; Payton et al., 2008; Pontiz, McClelland, Matthews & Morrison, 2009; Malik, 2008; Pelco & Reed-Victor, 2007; Bodrova & Leong, 2005) and most conclude that children without such skills are at risk for numerous school and life difficulties (Jones, Greenberg & Crowley, 2015; Jacobson, Williford & Pianta, 2011; Dawson & Guare, 2010; Pontiz et al., 2009; Blair & Diamond, 2008; Payton et al., 2008; Pelco & Reed-Victor, 2007; Bodrova & Leong, 2005; Eisenberg, Smith, Sadovsky & Spinrad, 2004; McCabe et al., 2004). One takes the compelling stand that "instruction in self-regulation in the early years deserves the same—if not more—attention as instruction in academic subjects" (Bodrova & Leong, 2005, p. 57).

For children who lack self-regulation and control, risk beyond the school years is extremely concerning (Jones et al., 2015). In a report on the proceedings of the National Academy of Sciences studying 1,000 children over 30 years, self-control, defined as the ability to "delay gratification, control impulses, modulate emotional expression" (Moffit, et al., 2010, p. 1), is critical to life success. Lack of mastery predicted worrisome futures beyond school such as crime, addiction, incarceration, and poor physical and mental health. Baumeister and Tierney (2011), who comprehensively report on self-control research, conclude: "The results couldn't be clearer: Self-control is a vital strength and key to success in life" (p.13).

Teaching the self-regulation of learning-related social skills has historically been done through "modeling, role playing and acknowledging examples of positive student behavior" (Pelco & Reed-Victor, 2007, p. 41). The executive summary by the Collaborative for Academic, Social and Emotional Learning (CASEL) comprehensively reviewed the impact of over 300 social/emotional learning programs and concluded that effective teaching practices for such skill mastery should be "sequenced, active, focused and explicit (SAFE)" (Payton et al., 2008, p. 6). More current research indicates that the SAFE model "affects central executive cognitive function such as inhibitory control, planning, and set shifting that are the result of building greater cognitive-affect regulation in prefrontal areas of the cortex" (Durlak, Weissberg, Dymnicki, Taylor & Schellinger, 2011, p. 6) and ensures children will move from the need for external supports to "internalized beliefs and values, caring and concern for others, making good decisions and taking responsibility for one's choices" (p. 2). The literature also recognizes that "teaching involves others providing instruction and guidance, but for self-regulation to develop, this external influence must be internalized by learners into their self-regulatory systems" (Schunk, 2008, p. 466).

But how, explicitly, is this internalization taught to and mastered by children, especially young ones? The above research supports the need for instruction of self-regulation of learning-related social skills, with recommendations for general teaching practices for skill mastery. Yet I was seeking something more fundamental: An explicit approach to developing this internal self-awareness and the mind-body states that would encourage self-regulation to develop and would be effectively generalizable for even our youngest children. I was supported in this inquiry by the developing interest in teaching these states and skills by utilizing the body, the mind, and the breath to more comprehensively practice the "effortful control" (Eisenberg et al., 2004, p. 259) and positive learning states (Shanker, 2013; Jensen, 2003) numerous learning-related social skills demand (Committee for Children, 2016; Carpenter, 2012; White, 2009; Galantino, Galbavy & Quinn, 2008; Malik, 2008; Slovacek, Tucker & Pantoja, 2003).

The field of yoga, which requires children to engage their bodies, minds, and breath simultaneously through movement (Flynn, 2012; Mailk, 2008; Slovacek et al., 2003; Kalish & Guber, 2001) and the field of mindfulness, which requires children to bring focused attention without judgment to tasks (Hawn Foundation, 2011; Gregory, 2009; Hooker & Fodor, 2008; Siegel, 2007), have offered me the best tools for teaching optimal states for self-regulation of these social skills in the most explicit way. I sought extensive training through the 200-hour Kripalu Yoga Teacher Training (2008) and 40-hour YogaEd Curriculum Training (2010) and have a well-established personal practice which enabled me to competently integrate this field into my teaching. Research on these practices is in its infancy, but studies with children and in schools are increasing, and though conclusions are often general, have provided promising results (Ferreira-Vorkapic et al., 2015; Chen & Pauwels, 2014; Khalsa, Hickley-Schultz, Cohen, Steiner & Cope, 2011; Noggle, Steiner, Minami & Khalsa, 2012). To contribute to the field myself, I conducted an action research pilot study at my school site on the *Calm and Alert* class (McGlauflin, 2010), which sought feedback from both parents and teachers, and also had a social work intern conduct a case study of its effectiveness (Perkins, 2015).

Articles that discuss teaching yoga skills to children have shown general promise in offering children explicit tools for being "calm and alert," but attempt to measure a wide range of variables. Variables include, but are not limited to, improvements in health, well-being and mood (Khalsa & Butzer, 2016; Chen & Pauwels, 2014; Pandit & Satish, 2014; Flynn, 2012; Noggle et al., 2012; Serwacki & Cook-Cottone, 2012; Crowley, 2002); academic achievement and school success (Chen & Pauwels, 2014; Serwacki & Cook-Cottone, 2012; Carpenter, 2012; Buckenmeyer & Freitas, 2007; Manjunath & Telles, 2004; Slovacek et al., 2003; Augenstein, 2003; Kalish & Guber, 2001); self-regulation (Steiner, Sidhu, Pop, Frenette & Perrin, 2013; McGlauflin, 2010; Malik, 2008; Augenstein, 2003); and stress reduction (Chen & Pauwels, 2014; Frank, Bose & Schrobenhauser-Clonan, 2014; Carpenter, 2012; Khalsa et al., 2011). A few studies attempt to examine yoga's effects on attention for students with such deficits (Peck, Kehle, Bray & Theodore, 2005; Jensen & Kenney, 2004). Most share a hope that bringing yoga practices to youth will "afford them the tools to lead successful, healthy and happy lives" (Serwacki & Cook-Cottone, 2012, p. 106), or take a strong stand that "yoga is an important life skill tool for children and young people to cope with stress and self-regulation in a life-long perspective" (Hagen & Nayar, 2013, p. 3). Although the research is nascent, personal accounts from practitioners like myself—who see skills generalized and self-regulation improve—can be powerful (Perkins, 2015; McGlauflin, 2010).

I have selected the safest and least controversial aspects from the yoga field to bring to the *Calm and Alert* practices. These include a deep respect for teaching and learning, creating a partnership between teacher and child; the instruction in, and practice of, mindful movement and conscious breathing; the relaxed, calming atmosphere the practices encourage; the imagery from nature; the partnership between body, mind, and breath; and the principles of healthy exertion and rest. Throughout the practice, children should be happy and relaxed even when challenged, their minds and bodies feeling free. These elements from the yoga field have been more enjoyable to the children and more effective instruction than I ever imagined.

Articles and books that discuss teaching mindfulness to children also show general promise in offering students concrete tools (meditation, breathing exercises, instruction about how the brain works) to be conscious of their bodies and minds and develop self-regulation. These teachings are also easily implemented in a home or school setting (Semple & Droutman, 2017; Vickery & Dorjee, 2016; Neiman, 2015; Hawn Foundation, 2011; Schoeberlein, 2009; Napoli, Krech & Holley, 2008). Research reports improvements for children with the practice of mindfulness skills, in areas of overall health (Cullen, 2011), school success (Vickery & Dorjee, 2016; Hawn Foundation, 2012; Tadlock-Marlo, 2011), self-regulation (Weare, 2013; Zelazo & Lyons, 2011; Singh et al., 2010; Semple, Reid & Miller, 2005), attention (Burdick, 2016; Burke, 2010; Hooker & Fodor, 2008; Naploi, Krech & Holley, 2005), anxiety reduction (Semple et al., 2005), prevention of self-harm (Britton et al., 2014); on-task behavior in the classroom (Carboni, Roach & Fredrick, 2013), and improved executive function (Flook et al., 2010). There appear to be few to no risks reported with such practices and most are found enjoyable to students (Weijer-Bergsma, Langenberg, Brandsma, Oort & Bogels, 2012; Hawn Foundation, 2011; Burke, 2010; Malik, 2008), though the infancy of the research makes definitive conclusions difficult (Semple & Droutman, 2017). This field also offers research support that mindfulness practices can help reduce stress for teachers and other adults (Meiklejohn et al., 2012; Gold et al., 2010) and thereby offer benefits for the children they serve.

I have also selected the safest and least controversial aspects from the mindfulness field to bring to the *Calm and Alert* practices, such as the benefits of utilizing the breath for creating calm and alert states, noticing the workings of the mind, attention and focus skills, and teaching children about their brains. The beauty of the mindfulness practices is that they do not require movement for adults who are not confident, and they are easy to implement in any setting. A few conscious breaths can be done anywhere, attentional strategies are useful for any task, and children enjoy learning and talking about the workings of the brain.

Calm and Alert was designed to utilize the SAFE standards and the best, most appropriate aspects of yoga and mindfulness in order to engage children's minds, bodies, and breath to create optimal body and minds states for the self-regulation needed to master a variety of social skills. When aspects of yoga and mindfulness have been utilized they appear practically in the instruction of movement and flow, and learning the landscape of our minds. From SAFE I have ensured the practices are:

1. Sequenced: As outlined in the chapters, skills can build on one another.
2. Active: The learning involves movement and the awareness of the body.
3. Focused: Children are fully engaged and are taught how to engage and focus in each area.
4. Explicit: Skills are clearly defined, expectations clearly stated in each area, and movements/breathwork are taught step by step.

My priority has been to create concepts and define skills that are firmly grounded in the research from relevant fields. The terms "calm and alert" are found at regular intervals in the literature, recognized as optimal states for best learning and functioning (Shanker, 2013; Jensen & Kenny, 2004; Kalish & Guber, 2001). Recognizing the importance of establishing program core components (Gould, Dariotis, Greenberg & Mendelson, 2015), *Calm and Alert* offers six concept/unit areas (respect, calm, alert, learning times, transition times, social times) for instruction. The *Calm and Alert* terms have been noncontroversial and comfortable for children and adults, and the six unit areas comprehensive and sensible. See Chapter 8 for more information regarding the noted benefits of the program.

References

Altman, D. (2014). *The Mindfulness Toolbox.* Eau Claire, WI: PESI Media and Publishing.

Augenstein, S. (2003). Yoga for children in primary school—An empirical study. *Journal for Meditation and Meditation Research, 3,* 27–44.

Baumeister, R. & Tierney, J. (2011). *Willpower.* New York: Penguin Press.

Blair, C. & Diamond, A. (2008). Biological processes and intervention: The promotion of self-regulation as a means of preventing school failure. *Development and Psychopathology, 20,* 899–911. DOI: 10.1017/S0954579408000436.

Bodrova, E. & Leong, D. (2005). Promoting student self-regulation in learning. *Principal, 71*(2), 54–57.

Britton, W. B., Lepp, N. E., Niles, H. F., Rocha, T., Fisher, N. E. & Gold, J. S. (2014). A randomized controlled pilot of classroom-based mindfulness meditation compared to an active control condition in sixth-grade children. *Journal of School Psychology, 52,* 263–278.

Buckenmeyer, J. & Freitas, D. (2007). Factors affecting student achievement and related behaviors. Retrieved from: http://www.yogakidsofcny.com/ToolsForSchools2.htm.

Burdick, D. (2016). *ADHD: Non-Medication Treatment & Skills For Children and Teens.* Eau Claire, WI: PESI Media and Publishing.

Burke, C. (2010). Mindfulness-based approaches with children and adolescents: A preliminary review of current research in an emergent field. *Journal of Child and Family Studies, 19,* 133–144. DOI: 10.1007/s10826-009-9282x.

Butzer, B., Ebert, M., Telles, S. & Khalsa, S. B. (2015). School-based yoga programs in the United States: A survey. *Advances, 29*(4), 18–26.

Byrnes, K. (2009). *Portraits of contemplative teaching* (Unpublished doctoral thesis). University of Colorado.

Carboni, J., Roach, A. & Fredrick, L. (2013). Impact of mindfulness training on the behavior of elementary students with attention-deficit/hyperactive disorder. *Research in Human Development, 10*(3), 234–251. DOI: 10.1080/15427609.2013.818487.

Carpenter, K. (2012). *Take Your Body to School: Yoga and Mindfulness are Universal Supports for Behavior, Achievement and Health.* Unpublished manuscript.

Cash, R. (2016). *Self-Regulation in the Classroom: Helping Students Learn How to Learn.* Golden Valley, MN: Free Spirit Publishing.

Chen, D. D. & Pauwels, L. (2014). Perceived benefits of incorporating yoga into classroom teaching: Assessment of the effects of "yoga tools for teachers." *Advances in Physical Education, 4,* 138–148. http://dx.doi.org/10.4236/ape.2014.43018.

Childress, T. & Cohen-Harper, J. (Eds.). (2015). *Best Practices for Yoga in the Schools.* Atlanta, GA: Yoga Service Council/Omega Publications.

Cohen-Harper, J. (2013). *Little Flower Yoga for Kids.* Oakland, CA: New Harber Publications.

Committee for Children. (2016). Second Step Curriculum, Seattle, WA. Retrieved from: http://www.cfchildren.org/second-step/social-emotional-learning.

Cowley, A. (2002). *The psychological and physiological effects of yoga on children* (Unpublished master's thesis). School of Social and Behavioral Sciences, Swineburne University of Technology, Hawthorne, Victoria, Australia.

Cullen, M. (2011). *Mindfulness Based Interventions: An Emerging Field.* Springer Science and Business Media, LLC. DOI: 10.1007/s12671-011-0058-1.

Davidson, R. (2013). *The Emotional Life of Your Brain.* London: Penguin Books.

Dawson, P. & Guare, R. (2010). *Executive Skills in Children and Adolescents.* New York: The Guilford Press.

Durlak, J., Weissberg, R., Dymnicki, A., Taylor, R. & Schellinger, K. (2011). The impact of enhancing students' social and emotional learning: A meta-analysis of school based universal interventions. [Special issue]. *Child Development, Raising Healthy Children, 82*(1), 405–432. DOI: 10.1111/j.1467-8624.2010.01564.x.

Eisenberg, N., Smith, C., Sadovsky, A. & Spinrad, T. L. (2004). Effortful control. In R. F. Baumeister & K. D. Vohs (Eds.), *Handbook of Self-Regulation,* pp. 259–282. New York: The Guilford Press.

Ferreira-Vorkapic, C., Feitoza, J. M., Marchioro, M., Simões, J., Kozasa, E. & Telles, S. (2015). Are there benefits from teaching yoga at schools? A systematic review of randomized control trials of yoga-based interventions. *Evidence-Based Complementary and Alternative Medicine,* Vol 2015, 1–17, Article ID 345835, http://dx.doi.org/10.1155/2015/345835.

Flook, L., Smalley, S., Kitil, M., Gall, B., Kaiser-Greenland, S., Locke, J., Ishijima, E. & Kasari, C. (2010). Effects of mindful awareness practices on executive function in elementary school children. *Journal of Applied School Psychology, 26*(1), 70–95. DOI: 10.1080/15377900903379125.

Flynn, L. (2012). Yoga 4 Classrooms. Retrieved from: http://www.yoga4classrooms.com.

Frank, J. L., Bose, B. & Schrobenhauser-Clonan, A. (2014). Effectiveness of a school-based yoga program on adolescent mental health, stress coping strategies, and attitudes toward violence: Findings from a high-risk sample. *Journal of Applied School Psychology, 30*(1), 29.

Galantino, M. L., Galbavy, R. & Quinn, L. (2008). Therapeutic effects of yoga for children: A systematic review of the literature. *Pediatric Physical Therapy, 20*(1), 66-80. DOI: 10.1097/PEP.0b013e31815fl208.

Garland, T. (2016). *Hands-On Activities for Children with Autism & Sensory Disorders.* Eau Claire, WI: PESI Publishing and Media.

Gregory, B. M. (2009). *Cognitive Behavioral Treatment Manual.* Eau Claire, WI: PESI Publishing and Media.

Gold, E., Smith, A., Hopper, I., Herne, D., Tansey, G. & Hulland, C. (2010). Mindfulness-based stress reduction (MBSR) for primary school teachers. *Journal of Child and Family Studies, 19,* 184–189. DOI: 10.1007/s10826-009-9344-0.

Gould, L. F., Dariotis, K., Greenberg, M. & Mendelson, T. (2015). Assessing Fidelity of Implementation (FOI) for school-based mindfulness and yoga interventions: A systematic review. *Mindfulness,* original paper. DOI: 10.1007/s12671-015-0395-6.

Hagen, I. & Nayar, U. S. (2014). Yoga for children and young people's mental health and well-being: Research review and reflections on the mental health potentials of yoga. *Front Psychiatry, 5*(35), 1–6. DOI: 10.3389/fpsyt.2014.00035.

Hawn Foundation. (2011). *MindUP Curriculum.* New York: Scholastic.

Hooker, K. E. & Fodor, I. E. (2008). Teaching mindfulness to children. *Gestalt Review, 12*(1), 75–91.

Jacobson, L. A., Williford, A. P. & Pianta, R. C. (2011). The role of executive function in children's competent adjustment to middle school. *Psychology Press, 17*(3), 255–280. DOI: 10.1080/09297049.2010.535654.

Jensen, P. S. & Kenny, D. T. (2004). The effects of yoga on the attention and behavior of boys with attention-deficit hyperactivity disorder. *Journal of Attention Disorders, 7*(4), 205–216. DOI: 10.1177/10870547-0400700403.

Jenson, E. (2003). *Tools for Engagement.* Thousand Oaks, CA: Corwin Press.

Jones, D. E., Greenberg, M. & Crowley, M. (2015). Early social-emotional functioning and public health: The relationship between kindergarten social competence and future wellness. *American Journal of Public Health,* published online July, 2015. DOI: 10.2105/AJPH.2015.302630.

Kalish, L. & Guber, T. L. (2001). *YogaEd Tools for Teachers Manual.* Santa Monica, CA: YogaEd.

Kaunhoven, R. J. & Dorjee, D. (2017). How does mindfulness modulate self-regulation in preadolescent children? An integrative neurocognitive review. *Neuroscience and Biobehavioral Review, 74,* 163–184.

Khalsa, S. B. & Butzer, B. (2016). Yoga in school settings: A research review. *Annuls of the New York Academy of Sciences, 1373,* 45–55. DOI: 10.111/nyas.13025.

Khalsa, S. B., Hickley-Schultz, L., Cohen, D., Steiner, N. & Cope, S. (2011). Evaluation of the mental health benefits of yoga in secondary school: A preliminary randomized controlled Trial. *Journal of Behavioral Health Services and Research, 39*(1), 80–89. DOI: 10.1007/s11414-011-9249-8.

Kripalu Yoga Fellowship. (2008). *Kripalu Yoga Teacher Training Manual.* Stockbridge, MA: Kripalu Center for Yoga and Health.

Malik, J. (2008). *Adapting yoga to youngsters: Viewpoints of certified youth yoga teachers* (Doctoral dissertation). The California School of Professional Psychology. Retrieved from ProQuest (UMI No. 3303044).

Manjunath, N. K. & Telles, S. (2004). Spatial and verbal memory test scores following yoga and fine arts camp for school children. *Indian Journal of Physio-Pharmacology, 48*(3), 353–356.

McCabe, L. A., Cunnington, M. & Brooks-Gunn, J. (2004). The development of self-regulation in young children. In R. F. Baumeister & K. D. Vohs (Eds.), *Handbook of Self-Regulation,* pp. 340–356. New York: The Guilford Press.

McClelland, M., Morrison, F. J. & Holmes, D. (2000). Children at risk for early academic problems: The role of learning-related social skills. *Early Childhood Research Quarterly, 15*(3), 307–329.

McGlauflin, H. (2010). The calm and alert class: Using mind, body and breath to teach the self-regulation of learning-related social skills. Educational Resource Information Center, ED511066. Retrieved from: http://www.eric.ed.gov.

Meiklejohn, J., Phillips, C., Freedman, M., Griffin, M., Beigal, G., Roach, A., Frank, J., Burke, C., Pinger, L., Soloway, G., Isberg, R., Sibinga, E., Grossmana, L. & Saltzman, A. (2012). Integrating mindfulness training into K-12 education: Fostering the resilience of teachers and students. *Mindfulness.* Advance online publication. DOI: 10.1007/s12671-012-0094-5.

Mind and Life Research Education Network (MLERN). (2012). Contemplative practices and mental training: Prospects for American education. *Child Development Perspectives*, 6, 146–153. DOI: 10.1111/j.1750- 8606.2012.00240.x.

Moffitt, T. E., Arseneault, L., Belsky, D., Dickson, N., Hancox, R., Harrington, H., Houts, R., Poulton, R., Roberts, B., Ross, S., Sears, M., Thomson, W. & Caspi, A. (2010). A gradient of childhood self-control predicts health, wealth and public safety. *Proceedings of the National Academy of the Sciences* (early edition), *108*(7), 1–6. Retrieved from: www.pnas.org/cgi/doi/10.1073/pnas.1010076108.

Naploi, M., Krech, P. & Holley, L. (2005). Mindfulness training for elementary school students: The attention academy. *Journal of Applied School Psychology*, *21*(1), 99–125. DOI: 10.1300/J370v21n01_05.

Neiman, B. (2015). *Mindfulness and Yoga Skills for Children and Adolescents.* Eau Claire, WI: PESI Publishing and Media.

Noggle, J. J., Steiner, N., Minami, T. & Khalsa, B. S. (2012). Benefits of yoga for psychological well-being in a U.S. high school curriculum: A preliminary randomized controlled trial. *Journal of Developmental Behavioral Pediatrics, 33*, 193–201.

Pandit, S. & Satish, L. (2014). When does yoga work? Long-term and short-term effects of yoga intervention among pre-adolescent children. *Psychological Studies*, *59*(2), 153–165. DOI: 10.1007/s12646-013-0209-7.

Payton, J., Weissberg, R. P., Durlak, J. A., Dymnicki, A. B., Taylor, R. D. & Schellinger, K. B. (2008). *The Positive Impact of Social and Emotional Learning for Kindergarten to Eighth Grade Students.* Collaborative for Academic and Social Emotional Learning. Retrieved from: www.casel.org.

Peck, H. L., Kehle, T. J., Bray, M. A. & Theodore, L. A. (2005). Yoga as an intervention for children with attention problems. *School Psychology Review*, *34*(3), 415–424.

Pelco, L. E. & Reed-Victor, E. (2007). Self-regulation and learning-related social skills: Intervention ideas for elementary school students. *Preventing School Failure*, *51*(3), 36–43. Retrieved from ProQuest, No. 1045988x.

Perkins, S. (2015). *Case study of calm and alert: Teacher reflections on a mind-body school-based intervention at Woodside Elementary in Topsham, Maine* (Unpublished master's thesis). University of New England.

Pontiz, C. C., McClelland, M. M., Matthews, J. S. & Morrison, F. J. (2009). A structured observation of behavioral self-regulation and its contribution to kindergarten outcomes. *Developmental Psychology*, *45*(3), 605–619. DOI: 10.1037/a0015365.

Rogers, V. W. & Motyka, E. (2009). 5-2-1-0 Goes to school: A pilot project testing the feasibility of schools adopting and delivering healthy messages during the school day. *Pediatrics*, *123*(5), S272–276. Downloaded from pediatrics.aappublications.org by guest on January 28, 2015. DOI: 10.1542/peds.2008-2780E.

Saltzman, A. (2012). *Mindfulness: A Guide for Teachers.* Retrieved from: stillquietplace.com.

Schoeberlein, D. (2009). *Mindful Teaching, Teaching Mindfulness.* Boston, MA: Wisdom Publications.

Schunk, D. H. (2008). Metacognition, self-regulation, and self-regulated learning: Research recommendations. *Educational Psychology Review, 20*, 463–467. DOI: 10.1007/s10648-008-9086.

Semple, R., Lee, J., Rosa, D. & Miller, L. (2010). A randomized trial of mindfulness-based cognitive-behavioral therapy for children: Promoting mindful attention to enhance social-emotional resiliency in children. *Journal of Child and Family Studies, 19,* 218–229. DOI: 10.1007/s10826-009-9301-y.

Semple, R., Reid, E. & Miller, L. (2005). Treating anxiety with mindfulness: An open trial of mindfulness training for anxious children. *Journal of Cognitive Psychotherapy, an International Quarterly, 19*(4), 379–392.

Semple, R. & Droutman, V. (2017). Mindfulness goes to school: Things learned from research and real-world experiences. *Psychology in Schools, 54*(1), 29–51. DOI: 10.1002/pits.

Serwacki, M. L. & Cook-Cottone, C. (2012). Yoga in schools: A systematic review of the literature. *International Journal of Yoga Therapy, 22,* 101–109.

Shanker, S. (2013). *Calm, Alert and Learning.* Toronto: Pearson Canada, Inc.

Siegel, D. J. (2007). *The Mindful Brain.* New York: W.W. Norton and Co.

Singh, N., Singh, A., Lancioni, G., Singh, J., Winton, A. & Adkins, A. (2010). Mindfulness training for parents and their children with ADHD increase children's compliance. *Journal of Child and Family Studies, 19,* 157–166.

Slovacek, S., Tucker, S. A. & Pantoja, L. (2003). *A Study of the YogaEd Program at the Accelerated School.* (Program Evaluation and Research Collaborative.) Retrieved from: www.calstatela.edu/academic/ccoe/c_perc/c_perc.

Sokol, B. W., Grouzet, F. & Muller, U. (Eds.). (2013). *Self-Regulation and Autonomy.* New York: Cambridge University Press.

Steiner, N., Sidhu, T., Pop, P., Frenette, E. & Perrin, E. (2013). Yoga in an urban school for children with emotional and behavioral disorders: A feasibility study. *Journal of Child and Family Studies, 22,* 815–826. DOI: 10.1007/s10826-012- 9636-7.

Sternberg, M. (1998). *American Sign Language Dictionary.* New York: Harper Collins.

Tadlock-Marlo, R. (2011). Making minds matter: Infusing mindfulness into school counseling. *Journal of Creativity in Mental Health, 6,* 220–233. DOI: 10.1080/15-401383.2011.605079.

Van der Kolk, B. (2014). *The Body Keeps Score.* New York: Penguin Group.

Vickery, C. E. & Dorjee, D. (2016). Mindfulness training in primary schools decreases negative affect and increases meta-cognition in children. *Frontiers in Psychology, 6.* DOI: 10.3389/fpsyg.2015.02025.

Weare, K. (2013). Developing mindfulness with children and young people: A review of the evidence and policy context. *Journal of Children's Services, 8*(2), 141–153. DOI: 10.1108/JCS-12-2012-0014.

Weijer-Bergsma, E., Langenberg, G., Brandsma, R., Oort, F. & Bogels, S. (2012). The effectiveness of school-based mindfulness training as a program to prevent stress in elementary school children. *Mindfulness, 5,* 238–248. DOI: 10.1007/s12671-012-0171-9.

White, L. S. (2009). Yoga for children. *Pediatric Nursing, 35*(5), 277–295.

Zelazo, P. & Lyons, K. (2011). Mindfulness training in childhood. *Human Development, 54,* 61–65. DOI: 10.1159/000327548.

Zenner, C., Hermleben-Kurz, S. & Walach, H. (2014). Mindfulness-bases interventions in schools—a systematic review and meta-analysis. *Frontiers in Psychology, 5,* Article 603, 1–20. DOI: 10.3389/fpsyg.2014.0063.